THE MODERN ENTREPRENEUR'S GUIDE TO SUCCESS

BUILDING A SUSTAINABLE BUSINESS IN THE 21ST CENTURY

LENA VOSS

Table of Contents

INTRODUCTION:
A Little Change Is Good

In this fast-moving business environment, innovation is a driver of growth and disruption, and an entrepreneurial mindset will be a shining beacon of ingenuity and adaptability. *"The Modern Entrepreneur's Guide to Success: Building a Sustainable Business in the 21st Century"* is an enlightening guide to decode the intricate balance between inspiration, resilience, and mental health that goes into achieving business success. As we delve into the significance of entrepreneurship, it becomes evident that this mindset not only shapes our world but also significantly impacts individual success and satisfaction.

Business is way more than creating wealth or developing companies; it's the very innate drive behind international innovation and economic development. This is what entrepreneurs act to do: catalyze growth, job creation, and wealth generation. Business thrives on innovation and trial and error. It embraces risks and challenges the status quo by pushing out the boundaries of what may be achieved. With an ever-changing global economy, entrepreneurship becomes another source of strength and an agent for change, engendering growth and success across markets and regions. At the heart of the entrepreneurial journey lies the motivation—a potent force—to look beyond present limitations for opportunities, to proceed ahead with bold choices for ambitious goals, and to persist in the face of adversity.

In *"The Modern Entrepreneur's Guide to Success: Building a Sustainable Business in the 21st Century,"* we explore sources of motivation and ways to succeed on an entrepreneurial journey that comes with its highs and lows. After setting goals and drawing up a growth mindset, you will go into an innovative journey to unlock that inner motivation and put it to practice in realizing your business dreams. But motivation isn't enough to guide one through the rough waters of entrepreneurship. In an environment where uncertainty and incessant change prevail, resilience is a landmark characteristic that underpins corporate success. It allows entrepreneurs to bounce back from anything unfavorable, adapt to change, and remain persistent without wavering on the vision. A period of misfortune or failure will be accepted and learned from, getting one back on their feet even more robust with more resolve. This book will take you on an involuntary journey to develop resilience through the eyes of psychology and neuroscience, powered by real-life examples, to journey equipped with a mindset and tools ready to successfully go through the highs and lows that entrepreneurship will throw at you.

The entrepreneurial effort also underscores mental health as the basis by which strength, stability, and growth would be provided to entrepreneurs to flourish despite organizational stressors and uncertainties. The demands of entrepreneurship can put a significant strain on your psychological wellness, leading to tension, burnout, and exhaustion. Thus, in every course taken and thought embarked on, taking care of one's psyche is important not just for personal satisfaction but also for sustaining business success. With *"The Modern Entrepreneur's Guide to Success: Building a Sustainable Business in the 21st Century,"* you can learn how to take care of your psyche in order to be more resilient, creative, and productive in your business.

In addition, you will learn how to critically assess and cultivate the requisite business mindset that can enable you to be a performer both in terms of leadership and as an individual. This amazing book is structured into thirteen insightful chapters that offer the reader a complete overview of the entrepreneurial journey and techniques actually to use in order to pursue success.

From laying the groundwork of entrepreneurship to innovation, hurdling challenges, preparing for disruption, building resilience and creativity, effective leadership, and partnership, everything is chock-full of information and insight that matches your empowering mindset and skills, which will lead you toward striving for business excellence. This book has also directed one's focus on the importance of managing the levels of anxiety and psychological well-being to steer it towards health and well-being to boost entrepreneurial strength and efficiency. *"The Modern Entrepreneur's Guide to Success: Building a Sustainable Business in the 21st Century"* not only imparts knowledge and skills for business success but also instills the mindset and resilience of viable success in the face of uncertainty. This authoritative guide is essential if you are a determined business owner who wants to launch your first venture or an experienced entrepreneur who wants to take your business to a higher level. It provides insight into the journey towards successful business and greater scalability. Its clear structure and inestimable insights make this book a source of practical advice and valuable resources—tools and techniques—to move with assurance and strength through the complexities of entrepreneurship. This book shows you the possibilities that lie before you as a business owner, as well as a pioneer of change in an ever-changing world.

CHAPTER 1:
The Entrepreneurial Mindset

Welcome to the first chapter of this book. In this chapter, we look at the multi-faceted concept of entrepreneurship and what it really means to be entrepreneurial. We will learn about the various views of entrepreneurship and the characteristics that successful entrepreneurs have in common. This chapter brings out what entrepreneurship is really about, not just profit-making but also the goals of creation, innovation, and making a difference. We will probe the traits pivotal to entrepreneurial success and how these attributes of individuals translate into actualizing their vision. By knowing the core principles and motivations of entrepreneurship, you will know what is needed to circumnavigate the challenges and also seize the advantages that this dynamic journey offers.

People have different opinions on what entrepreneurship means to them. This influences their willingness to use the tag 'entrepreneur'. There is no doubt that there is a prestige that comes with being called one, as there are woes. I have heard people in several rooms say that to be an entrepreneur, you must have the 'hustling spirit'. In that statement, I always imagine someone who does not back down but remains committed to success against all odds. While this is my personal perspective, it would be helpful to consider what others have said in this regard.

What Is Entrepreneurship?

Entrepreneurship is about the identification of business-related opportunities, which involves recognizing and acting on potential ventures that can create value. (Smith, J., & Doe, A., 2019). This could be done by an individual or, a small group or partners. Whether you are starting out as an individual or as part of a partnership, you should recognize that entrepreneurship is about originality. It is about creating a new product or service or improving an existing one. A brooding thought in the mind of an entrepreneur is, 'How can things be done differently?'

In the United States, it was reported that 5,481,437 new businesses were commenced in 2023. This implies that, in 2023, millions of individuals took the initiative to introduce innovative products and services into the market. You might be one of such individuals who has a product in the market or intends to introduce one in the nearest feature. If you belong to the latter, this is your cue to get started.

Entrepreneurship could take different forms—venture capital-backed startups, corporate entrepreneurship, small business, and the list goes on. I would says that the common denominator is the willingness of entrepreneurs to recognize opportunities even when the path is unclear. These individuals are able to mobilize resources to pioneer change in their respective industries.

I will take a pause here to say that the scope of entrepreneurship is wide enough to include individuals who may not necessarily be interested in starting a business but have the desire to create initiatives that contribute to a greater purpose. It is a process where people search for the intersection of their abilities and the needs of others, as entrepreneurship is about introducing innovations into a community and having a keen understanding and appreciation of the needs and desires of community members (Korte et al., 2018). It is about asking ourselves, 'How can I use what I have to better the lives of others?' When we are able to not only discover the answer but implement this answer, then we inadvertently become a part of the value creation team. In return, people are willing to give money in exchange for our products or services that solve their problems. At all times, the goal is to ensure that the value is proportional to the monetary reward. Where it is not, then an entrepreneur is said to have suffered a loss.

Why Do People Start Businesses?

At the heart of a successful business is usually an entrepreneur with a clear idea. Often described as an 'itch' that needs to be scratched, entrepreneurs are characterized by an overriding need to act. It is this need that drives their passion and the other qualities of an entrepreneurial mindset.

From GEM's 2023 survey of new business founders as to the specific reasons for starting a business, it was found that the majority of the respondents in the United States started their business to build great wealth or very high income or a desire to make a difference in the world (about 64 percent), or to earn a living due to scarcity of jobs, and to continue a family tradition. There are other reasons people start businesses, including the drive to find a solution. I am aware that many people also express dissatisfaction with working for someone else – claiming they could do a better job or their heart isn't in it. In truth, though, 'someone else's dream' can act as a strong motivator for individuals to try their own business—using the experience and contacts they have gained to create their own success. This is partly explained by the Theory of Planned Behavior by Ajzen in 1991, which shows that the intention to start a business is a result of attitude, subjective norms, and perceived behavioral control. Those who seek control and consider starting a business as a clear-cut path to their goal, taking into account the people whose opinions they value, will generally have a strong reason to start a business.

The survey also recognized that exiting a business is a minority activity, with less than one in 20 adults involved in 26 of the 45 economies that the survey covered. In some exit cases, the businesses were sold to another entrepreneur. This implies that the business itself remains a going concern and continues to contribute to the nation's economy.

Significance of Entrepreneurship in Economic Growth

Entrepreneurship works as a stimulant for economic growth, playing an essential role in driving advancement, creating job opportunities, and promoting total economic development. This is why entrepreneurship is important for economic growth:

- **Innovation**: Entrepreneurs are at the center of innovation in any market. They bring new products, services, and processes to the market. They identify gaps and come up with solutions that people are willing to buy. By doing so, it directly results in economic growth.

- **Employee Opportunities**: Entrepreneurial activities are the main source of job opportunities in the world today. Small-scale and local companies also tend to be the employers, absorbing a large portion of the labor market especially in developing countries. By the merit of employing people and equally providing them with opportunities to involve in the business world, entrepreneurs reduce unemployment and thus poverty.

- **Wealth Generation**: Entrepreneurship becomes successful in creating wealth not only for the entrepreneurs themselves but also for society in general. Through successful ventures, entrepreneurs create wealth, draw capital, acquire new ventures, and generate added economic activity. Such created wealth is circulated throughout the whole economy, enhances success, and brings up the quality of life of communities.

- **Regional Development**: Entrepreneurship can work as an impetus to regional development, especially in underdeveloped or backward areas. Entrepreneurs will set up business units in such areas to improve regional economic status, mobilize investment, and bring infrastructural development. This decentralizes economic activity, contributing to a more even distribution of wealth and resources.

- **Improved Productivity and Competitiveness**: Through entrepreneurship, it encourages competition and organizations are forced to be better at being effective and efficient. This is because with the fact that entrepreneurs will come up with ways to ensure that their products are different and also gain a market competitive advantage; they must be able to sustain this through research and investment in modern technology as well as in new skills. It is in this understanding that performance, in general, across markets has greatly improved, hence making global economic markets much more competitive.

- **Resilience and Adaptability**: Entrepreneurial activities are by nature dynamic and flexible. Business owners deal with uncertainties, knock down barriers, and take advantage of existing opportunities amidst changing market conditions. This builds financial security from more income streams and, in turn, reduces the possibility of risk that might come from dependency on a few markets or income sources.

- **International Integration**: Entrepreneurship is a significant contribution to globalization because entrepreneurs engage in cross-border international trade and cross-border investment of their finances. Businesspeople often venture into the international arena by exporting and importing goods and services, partnering in cross-border investment opportunities and giving judiciary leadership across borders. This is likely to create inter-connected economies, propels multi-cultural integration and further boosts business market potentials for a country.

Traits of an Entrepreneur

Entrepreneurs have a one-of-a-kind collection of attributes that differentiate them from the basic populace. These qualities not only drive their success but also affect their decision-making, risk-taking personality, and the general mindset of an entrepreneur. Here are some vital features of business owners:

Passion

The passion that entrepreneurs exhibit can be infectious to those around them. It is not unusual for entrepreneurs to work 65-70 hours a week. The statement, "You will never do great work without doing a great deal of hard work," rings true for entrepreneurs. Because they are so passionate about their work, they will invest large amounts of time into their work, which is not perceived as "work" to them because they enjoy it so much. This, of course, can yield positive outcomes as the more time and effort invested in something, the bigger the potential return.

Entrepreneurs are not easily deterred by failure or mistakes. They view all experiences as lessons to learn from and grow in both their personal lives and business. As a result, the entrepreneur takes a laissez-faire attitude toward employees who are often very independent and share similar views on their work. Coming full circle, the entrepreneur is so passionate about his work that he will invest large amounts of time and effort into ventures with high probabilities of failure in hopes of the chance of success.

Risk-Taking Propensity

Entrepreneurs show a determination to take calculated risks in search of their objectives. They embrace venturing right into the unknown, welcoming unpredictability, notwithstanding the risks. Yet, they are well aware of the risks they take through full assessment, detailed research, and a calculated approach to handling unpredictability.

To further the argument, it is to be noted that entrepreneurship thrives on innovation and technology. In today's world, entrepreneurs have to master the art of thinking out of the box, which necessarily amounts to taking risks. They must come up with novel solutions, identify market opportunities, and design state-of-the-art solutions to address unmet needs. Whether it is innovative products or business designs, the entrepreneur takes one to the technological frontier.

Visionary Leadership

Entrepreneurs are basically innovators who believe in themselves and what they are doing. While others see restricting forces, they see opportunities; hence, others start believing in their vision with the developed motivators. Entrepreneurs demolish the barriers of resources through appropriate communication and tactical management and steer their efforts to success.

Of course, there are struggles in being an entrepreneur: barriers, problems, and, at times, failure. But unlike the investor, a businessman has the resiliency to continue just when the mistake occurs. He will rise from his fall, learn from errors, and adapt to changes. The same resilience will help him get over all the ups and downs of entrepreneurship and be all the stronger for having lived through it.

Adaptable and Flexible

Successful business owners practice flexibility and understand when it is important to change style and approach, subject to market conditions. They will rise to the challenge, pivot when it is necessary, and take advantage of new opportunities as those opportunities present themselves. By remaining proactive and open, business owners can allow themselves to navigate the complex and recognize the importance of networking in fostering business growth and opportunities. They use their network to access resources, develop strategic partnerships, and receive valuable information from mentors and fellow entrepreneurs. Effective networking enables entrepreneurs to broaden their reach, establish credibility, identify when to change their game plan, and, in turn, open the doors to new horizons.

Problem-Solving Skills

Entrepreneurs are good problem solvers; they have an excellent way of identifying problems, analyzing the source of the problem, and coming up with effective solutions. They approach challenges with a solution-oriented way of thinking, seeking ingenious methods to deal with complicated concerns and conquer challenges. Their problem-solving abilities allow them to navigate uncertainties and drive their endeavors toward success.

Growth Mindset vs. Fixed Mindset in Entrepreneurship

In the world of entrepreneurship, one's frame of mind plays an essential role in determining success. Mindsets are typically reviewed: the growth mindset and the fixed mindset. According to psychologist Carol Dweck, who was the first researcher to explore the idea of fixed and growth mindsets in her book *Mindset: The new psychology of success*. It is important to recognize the distinctions between these mindsets to thrive as a business owner.

A growth mindset is one that believes abilities and even intelligence can be developed through dedication, hard work, and learning. People with a mature mindset will see obstacles as growth potential and perceive failure as one of the paths to success. They take feedback well, remain resilient in the face of challenges, and become more motivated by the process of discovery in their field. Ideally, entrepreneurship should inculcate passion and a growth mindset, which easily takes risks, snatches opportunities, and makes solutions to counteract adverse circumstances. They are not stopped by adversities and have a high degree of motivation to continue innovating and growing his/her venture. A growth mindset is optimistic but not in an empty way. It is about being willing to put in the hard work and effort to get the results one believes are available.

A fixed mindset, on the other hand, is identified by the belief that abilities, together with one's intelligence, are part of someone's inherent nature—in other words, they cannot be changed. People with a fixed mindset have a tendency to avoid difficulties out of the feeling of inadequacy, as they view failure as a representation of their fundamental constraints. They might end up being stopped or limited by problems and tend to see the objection as an individual assault instead of a possibility for growth. In the context of entrepreneurship, those with a fixed mindset might avoid taking risks or seeking ambitious goals, going with a much safer and more foreseeable course. They might struggle to adjust to transforming market issues and might be much more resistant to feedback and innovations.

In life, people can have both a fixed and growth mindset in respect of different areas of their lives. You may find a person who believes that they can improve their profits if they master digital marketing and spend more money on advertising and the like. This same person could also simultaneously hold the belief that they are not good communicators and simply lack the talent to be one.

Opportunity Recognition and Pursuit

Effective business owners are willing and able to identify and profit from opportunities in the market. Opportunity recognition is the act of determining unmet demands, produce valuable returns. Nevertheless, identifying possibilities is just the very first step; business owners need to go after these opportunities with determination and tactical implementation.

- **Opportunity Recognition**: Business owners should proactively check their environment for opportunities by exploring and staying abreast with changes in customer choices, technical innovations, regulatory changes, and various other market characteristics. I recommend that entrepreneurs carry out market research to assess trends and engage potential consumers. This will enable entrepreneurs to determine lacunas and unmet needs. Business owners who accompany it with observation, creative thinking, and critical reasoning certainly identify opportunities that may be overlooked but are able to come forward with innovative alternatives at the same time as accompanying the journey toward profits.

- **Opportunity Pursuit:** Once they identify an opportunity, business entrepreneurs should act with decisiveness. This involves formulating a vision and strategy, mobilization of resources, as well as the use of the strategy with precision. I believe that entrepreneurs must be able to take risks, face challenges, and uncertainties while making their vision a concrete matter. The pursuit of opportunity thus requires that the entrepreneur be resilient, flexible, and willing to iterate on methods informed by feedback and customer/market needs.

As such, successful entrepreneurs are proactive in recognizing and seeking out new opportunities. By doing so, they seek to develop active initiatives that will make use of the available opportunities when they arise. Through the integration of creative thinking, critical thinking, and determination, business owners can open up the full potential of attractive opportunities while driving sustainable growth for their endeavors.

Proactiveness and Initiative

Proactiveness and effort are among the salient characteristics that clearly differentiate the most effective business owners from others. Proactive business owners take the initiative, put in effort, plan for difficulties, and even make a stride toward taking advantage or averting dangers.

- **Proactiveness**: Positive entrepreneurs are not the type of people to wait for opportunities to come their way. Instead, they are actively finding ways through which they can create value and drive development. They look forward to identifying market patterns and potential barriers and, at the same time, taking pre-emptive measures towards such. Positive entrepreneurs are so futuristic and as well calculative because they constantly keep researching in order to find ways through which they can introduce, guide performance, and stay ahead of their competitors.

- **Initiative**: Initiative means a wish to act without prompting and not waiting for specific orders. Go-getting business owners who deliver take full charge of their objectives and duties without waiting to be pushed. They are alert, independent, and compelled to make things happen. It is beyond any shadow of a doubt that entrepreneurship requires hard work, with success depending on translating one's own ideas into action and negotiating through a certain number of complex hurdles. It means being creative, resolute, and capable of making decisive choices.

Recognizing Success in Entrepreneurship

Success in entrepreneurship is more complex and involves various dimensions different from the financial success. As a component of a larger definition of business success, it's worth knowing what can comprise success in entrepreneurship: personal satisfaction, public impact, as well as long-term sustainability.

- **Financial Success**: Financial success is often the most visible evidence of business success, the one that people notice and can see. It is, too often, equated with being in business: "If you're not making money, then you're not a business," the logic goes. Some considerations in financial success are making money—profits— and making sure that your stakeholders share in the rewards that flow from your business. In this example, stakeholders would include business partners, employees, and business owners. Physical success also provides the resources for maintaining and growing the business, financing investments in growth, and paying for management and others working for the business.

- **Individual Fulfillment**: Satisfaction to many entrepreneurs is a passion through which energy is channeled and relationships built with individual values and goals. Individual satisfaction in entrepreneurship comes from the sense of building something meaningful: making an impact on other people, feeling freedom, competence, along with reaching their goals.

- **Public Impact**: Business success may also be measured by general impacts on society. Successful entrepreneurs not only create jobs but also have the capacity to initiate economic growth and even foster innovation. All of these elements contribute to success and overall growth in the various sectors of the economy. It champions the challenges of society and the environment and strengthens resilience, which then fortifies driving forces that increase the general well-being of the people and society in general.

- **Long-term Sustainability**: It is not about the quick buck; it's about long-term sustainability and prosperity. And indeed, successful entrepreneurs build for themselves flexible, wise businesses that will stand the test of time. Spend time learning them, foster a viable firm business culture, and provide for open and transparent service offerings that, when tested against challenges, turn out to be both resilient and strong.

CHAPTER 2:
The Psychology of Motivation

With the basic building blocks of the entrepreneurial mindset established in Chapter 1—where we uncovered pivotal traits and philosophies that underpin successful entrepreneurship—we now turn our attention to the core engine that powers any mindset: motivation. In this chapter, you will explore the psychology of motivation, delving into those drivers of entrepreneurship that push individuals toward transforming their vision into reality. So now we will go on and analyze both intrinsic and extrinsic factors that spark and continue the entrepreneurial spirit. Further, this chapter carries you through the neuroscience of motivation, revealing how brain functions influence our drive and persistence. It also elaborates on emotions' pivotal role in shaping motivation and decision-making. This chapter will give you deep insight into the mechanisms that allow entrepreneurs to stay inspired, focused, and capable of overcoming the sources of difficulty they will invariably face.

Motivation is the lifeblood of entrepreneurship and the spirit with which people overcome obstacles set in their way and attain success. The finer nuances of motivation in an ever-dynamic, ever-changing business world are what carve the course for becoming an ardent and indefatigable entrepreneur.

The Essence of Motivation

At its core, motivation is the internal drive that obliges people to act in the direction of accomplishing their goals. Whether it's introducing a start-up, establishing a brand-new item, or navigating the obstacles to excellent service delivery, motivation functions as the fuel that moves business owners ahead on their journey. Nevertheless, motivation is not a one-size-fits-all principle; it shows up in different kinds together and is affected by a myriad of elements.

Inherent Motivation: The Fire Within

Inherent motivation originates from inner wishes, enthusiasm, and level of interest. It's the natural desire to get involved in activities for the satisfaction and fulfillment derived from them. This is commonly referred to as 'intrinsic motivation'. For entrepreneurs, it often lies in some intrinsic interest in what they are doing or a true passion for their task of problem-solving or changing the world for the better.

Thus, another important characteristic of intrinsic motivation is autonomy: freedom to do what you love and care about to the extent that you want without external controls. Intrinsically motivated entrepreneurs are driven by their fluctuating passion for what they do. In working through the process, their satisfaction is gained rather than focusing solely on an end result at the conclusion of their venture. This intrinsic motivation encourages creativity, innovation, and a sense of worth and thus makes entrepreneurs push beyond their bounds and pursue their objectives with firm resolve.

External Motivation: Beyond the Rewards

On the other hand, external motivation is motivated by benefits or rewards from external sources. It is the assurance of tangible benefits or fear of negative consequences in general, such as economic benefits, formal recognition, or social circumstances.

Extrinsic motivation, though effective at some temporal spurts in increasing performance as well as efficiency, lacks the longevity and fulfillment that intrinsic motivation provides. Too much reliance on external rewards may tend to bring about superficial satisfaction and fulfillment, hence wearing off lasting motivation and engagement over time.

I might also mention here that the theory relative to intrinsic and extrinsic motivation is actually offshoots from the works of two behavioral personality psychologists who are using the approach in studying individual differences in behavioral self-regulation; they were Edward Deci and Richard Ryan.

Unraveling the Neuroscience of Motivation

Motivation, when viewed through a neuroscientific lens, carries with it vital data about the operations of the human mind and its response to various forms of stimuli. At the very core of inspiration lies a mesolimbic dopaminergic network, informally known as the dopamine reward center. When individuals do come into contact with rewarding or pleasurable stimuli, then there is a release of dopamine, and the signal is shot from the VTA to the accumbent.

Dopamine, the so-called "feel-good" neurotransmitter, is an

integral part of motivation to act by signaling expectation and receipt of reinforcement. In case we act in ways that are an accord with what we need and believe in, our brains will release some dopamine; such behaviors then get strengthened and motivate us to continue pursuing similar rewards in the future.

Inherent incentives play a role in triggering the brain's reward circuit. Tasks that provide a feeling of freedom, proficiency, and an objective activate the release of dopamine, cultivating internal motivation within an individual. On the other hand, external incentives might typically stop working to give long-term satisfaction—or satisfaction related to internal motivation. The frequency of dopamine neurons increases when a reward is better than expected and decreases when a reward is word than expected (Wang et al., 2020). This can be relied on to justify the demotivation that entrepreneurs encounter after suffering a loss.

The Influence of Emotions on Motivation and Decision-Making

Feelings play a considerable function in forming inspiration and decision-making processes. Favorable feelings such as enjoyment, happiness, and excitement can improve inspiration by invigorating people and enhancing their readiness to participate in goal-oriented habits. On the other hand, unfavorable feelings such as worry, anxiousness, and irritation can prevent inspiration and block decision-making by causing evasion habits and restricting cognitive sources.

Comprehending the impact of feelings on motivation can assist business owners in developing environments that foster favorable psychological experiences and lessen adverse ones. By promoting an encouraging and open-door office culture, giving chances for expression as well as social support, and applying techniques for handling stress, anxiety, and mishaps, business owners can improve the motivation level of their workers and the workers' well-being.

Inspirational States: Impact, Drive, and Mood

Inspirational states include a variety of experiences, drives, and moods that affect actions and decision-making. Impact describes the instant psychological action to stimulations; drive stands for the inner impulse or wishes to meet a demand or attain an objective or even state of mind while acknowledging and comprehending various inspirational states can assist business owners in customizing their management techniques as well as inspirational methods to fulfill the varied requirements of their staff members. By recognizing the impact of experiences, drives, and state of mind on motivation, business owners can develop encouraging environments that assist in the objective search, boost efficiency, and promote staff member's well-being.

The Role of Emotional Intelligence in Sustaining Motivation

Emotional Intelligence (EI) describes the ability to acknowledge, comprehend, and handle one's own feelings and those of others. The greater the level of EI, the more an individual can better manage his or her emotions effectively, influence others, and maneuver human relations.

Throughout a business context, EI keeps motivation alive while yielding positive work settings. An entrepreneur with high EI can build trust and vibrancy in his or her work teams by offering guidance, thoughtfully in time of uncertainty, and resolve conflicts constructively. With nurturing the development of skills in psychological knowledge reflected in a business environment, an entrepreneur makes some sort of assurance that the feelings will never be in their way whenever the big decisions have to be made.

Approaches for Emotion Regulation to Enhance Motivational Resilience

Emotional regulation can also describe the processes by which emotional experiences may be managed and balanced in such a way that individuals will adequately respond to challenging situations. The most successful tools of emotional regulation will be to keep individuals motivated and effective. On top of that, it can enhance the capacity for motivation, resilience, and well-being if the employees are helped to learn how to regulate their emotions. Mindful reflection and deep breathing exercises are among the available skills to help guide an individual's anxiety control and high emotions and instill positive expectations in situations full of uncertain change. Business owners who inculcate this level of resilience into their teams, coupled with determination and overall self-awareness and self-care, form an environment that is able to deal with challenges.

What Happens When You Lack Motivation?

A lack of motivation will have ruinous effects on the performance, creativity, and overall health of a business owner. When motivation diminishes, people may have an experience of:

1. **Lowered Productivity**: Without any driving force behind their activities, business owners might have a hard time concentrating and may not be able to complete jobs effectively, resulting in a decrease in efficiency.

2. **Loss of Creativity**: Motivation is fueled by innovation, and without inspiration, business owners might find it challenging to produce original ideas or solutions to problems, preventing development.

3. **Putting Things Off along with Avoidance**: An absence of inspiration can cause laziness and evasion actions as business owners might really feel overloaded or indifferent in tackling their duties.

4. **Raised Stress and Burnout**: Consistent absence of inspiration can add to enhanced anxiety as well as fatigue, as business owners might really feel overloaded by their work as well as demoralized by their lack of growth.

5. **Stagnation and Regression**: Without inspiration to drive them ahead, business owners run the risk of becoming bored or falling behind in their individual and professional growth, preventing

their ability to accomplish their objectives and passions.

Maintaining Motivation as a Business Owner

As business owners navigate the obstacles of a business, constant motivation is crucial for lasting success. Right here are some methods rooted in psychology and neuroscience to assist business owners in keeping their drive and energy:

1. **Cultivate Intrinsic Motivation**: Identify what really influences and encourages you. Straighten your business ventures with your core values and passions. Define clear, possible objectives that resonate with your internal motivations and give you a feeling of relevance and satisfaction.

2. **Harness Extrinsic Motivation Wisely**: Establish Rewards Strategically. Utilize external incentives as tools to enhance preferred actions and turning points. However, ensure that they enhance internal motivations as against overpowering it.

3. **Cultivate a Sense of Progress**: Divide bigger objectives into smaller, manageable tasks to develop a feeling of growth and success. In addition, monitor your success and commemorate your success. At all times, ensure that you use obstacles as opportunities for development and self-discovery.

4. **Welcome Challenges**: View difficulties and obstacles as opportunities for self- discovery and development as opposed to insurmountable challenges. Recognize that failure is an

inevitable part of the entrepreneurial journey and utilize it as a stepping stone toward future success.

5. **Find a New Perspective in an Unrelated Endeavor**: Sometimes, it could be helpful to seek a fresh experience by doing something new while reviewing your 'why' and cultivating intrinsic motivation. There is no doubt that the answer comes even when you are not looking. This could afford you the opportunity to discover a renewed passion for what you do and your target market.

Building Confidence Within Your Team

Building self-confidence within your group is critical for building motivation and producing a positive as well as efficient workplace. When staff member really feels great about themselves and their capabilities, they are more likely to handle brand-new difficulties, team up efficiently, and also contribute to the total success of the group. As a leader, it's your obligation to promote an environment where self-confidence can grow. Below are some techniques to help you build self-confidence in your group:

1. **Give Clear Expectations**: Plainly communicate your expectations to your employees. Ensure they understand their job description, duties, goals, and the ultimate mission of the organization. When staff members recognize what is expected of them, they are most likely to really feel great about their capacity to meet those expectations.

2. **Offer Support as well as Encouragement**: Let your employees know that you trust them and their capacities. Support and guide them, more so when they are in the process of doing new things or experiencing tough situations. Let them know that you can help them succeed and that you believe in their ability to do so.

3. **Commemorate Achievements**: Celebrate the achievements of your staff or overcome an obstacle; make an effort to acknowledge the struggle and achievement. Celebration will encourage the staff to put their best foot forward toward the job.

4. **Offer Opportunities for Growth**: Offer your employees opportunities to expand. Encourage them to take up new challenges, acquire new skills, and move out of their comfort zones. Opportunities for growth—not only in professional establishment but in growing resilience to succeed in all circumstances.

5. **Encourage Collaboration**: Make a collaborative workspace for employees to share ideas, ask questions, and ask one another for help. Encourage free communication and collaboration. This will foster an environment in which employees feel supported by their peers and are more.

6. **Provide Constructive Feedback**: Provide feedback that is constructive to your members so they can be aware of what they are doing well and what improvement areas need to be worked on. Help them set realistic goals for development and provide the necessary support and tools to achieve that goal. Constructive

feedback allows the team member to understand her development area and, in the process, enables self-confidence.

7. **Develop a Positive Work Environment**: Create a positive work environment where staff members really feel valued and appreciated. Encourage an open-door policy, promote a culture of partnership, and acknowledge the contributions of each employee. A positive work environment enhances motivation, causing higher efficiency and success.

8. **Provide Training and also Development Opportunities:** Secure the professional growth of your team members by providing training, workshops, and other learning opportunities. Assist them in establishing the abilities and expertise they require to do well in their roles and also excel in their jobs. When staff members feel supported in their professional growth, they are most likely to feel motivated.

9. **Be Accessible and Approachable**: Be friendly and easily accessible to your staff members. Encourage open interaction and offer to respond to inquiries, address problems, and also provide advice when required. When employee really feels comfortable coming to you for support and guidance, they are more likely to stay at their jobs.

CHAPTER 3:
Tricky Waters of Decision-Making

After journeying through the essentials of the entrepreneurial mindset and uncovering the deep-seated forces of motivation in the above chapters, you are now ready to tackle one of the most critical aspects of entrepreneurship—decision-making. So far, you have learned that adopting the right mindset lays the foundation for entrepreneurial success while knowing the psychology of motivation unleashes your motivation to carry you through difficulties. Elaborating on the foregoing, this chapter will take you through the subtle process of making decisions that may sometimes define the future course of your venture. The chapter looks at how you can apply models of rational and intuitive decision-making, each uniquely relevant to the complexities and ambiguities you will face. By learning how to navigate these tricky waters successfully, one is sure to steer his business with clarity and confidence by using his mindset and motivation to make fundamental choices aligning with the set vision and goals of the company.

Decision-making is a crucial aspect of business, which has a significant impact on the failure or success of a venture. There are a variety of decision-making designs. They offer business people diverse means of dealing with thorny issues and also making pivotal decisions. Among these are the Rational Decision-Making Model - based on deep analysis and logical argumentation - and the Intuitive Decision-Making Model based upon spontaneous impressions and intuition. These models guide the entrepreneur to find his way in the weeds by choosing a course of action - be it through pain-staking planning or quick reaction.

Rational Decision-Making Model

The rational decision-making design recommends that people make choices by very carefully examining choices, considering their repercussions, and picking the optimum selection based on reasoning as well as thinking. This design complies with an organized technique, including recognizing the challenge, event-appropriate details, reviewing options, and also picking the most effective choice. The rational decision-making design offers a structured strategy for business owners to make informed decisions in the middle of unpredictability. It motivates methodical evaluation, minimizing the chance of spontaneous choices.

Under this model, entrepreneurs start by acknowledging the requirement for a choice, commonly caused by obstacles, opportunities, or goals. They accumulate information as well as details connected to the choice consisting of market trends, customer choices and also monetary ramifications. The entrepreneur looks at the available alternatives, analyzing potential outcomes as well as risks. After analyzing, they select the alternative that is logical, or their business goals will support them in choosing the alternative that fits most reasonably.

Pros:

    a. Organized technique improves choice high quality.

    b. Helps with clear interaction and reason for choices.

    c. Ideal for choices with quantifiable results and enough details.

Cons:

    a. Presumes the best information and neglects psychological or user-friendly variables.

    b. Lengthy processes might not be reasonable in urgent situations.

    c. Overemphasis on evaluation might bring about choice paralysis.

Intuitive Decision-Making Model

Unlike the rational model, Intuitive decision-making relies on suspicion, premonitions, and responses as opposed to a systematic consideration of alternatives. This method is dependent on experiences of the past, implicit knowledge, and recognition of patterns that enable entrepreneurs always to make quick decisions when they find themselves in a situation that is not clear or uncertain. Intuitive management works in a dynamic and uncertain environment.

It makes organizations agile and adaptive, with quick responses to opportunities or threats.

In this model, entrepreneurs rely on earlier experience and information to find a pattern and similarity in current circumstances. Intuition usually involves consideration of psychological clues or unconscious messages that influence decision-making. Instead of full-blown analysis, entrepreneurs merely swallow the situation at hand and then apply intuition to tailor solutions to the problem.

Pros:

a. Quick decision-making fit to fast-changing environments.

b. Utilizes tacit expertise along with experience.

c. Reliable for choices with insufficient or uncertain

Cons:

a. Prone to predispositions and mistakes due to dependence on subjective judgments.

b. Hard to defend choices or clarify reasoning to others.

c. Might overlook vital information or forget long-lasting effects.

Behavioral Decision-Making Model

The behavioral decision-making design incorporates components of both rational and intuitive strategies, acknowledging that human choices are affected by cognitive predispositions, feelings, and social elements. This version recognizes the restrictions of reasonable or intuitive decision-making and seeks to recognize just how people, in fact, choose. Recognizing the behavioral facets of decision-making is vital for business owners to minimize predispositions, handle feelings, and leverage social impacts. Business owners can make even more rational and educated choices.

Under this model, entrepreneurs are vulnerable to numerous cognitive predispositions such as verification predisposition, anchoring prejudice, and overconfidence prejudice, which prejudice their judgment and decision-making. Further, emotions play a considerable function in decision-making, affecting risk assessment, motivation, and choices. External elements, consisting of social stress, social standards, and social impacts, form part of the decision-making process and also outcomes. There is a significant social focus when entrepreneurs evaluate solutions under this model.

Pros:

a. Incorporates insights from psychology and sociology right into decision-making.

b. Offers a much more reasonable representation of human decision-making processes

c. Provides approaches to alleviate predispositions and boost high-quality decision-making.

Cons:

   a. Complexity might make it tough to use in practice.

   b. Self-awareness and consideration are needed to acknowledge predispositions.

   c. Does not provide a prescriptive structure for decision-making.

Entrepreneurs adopt the above-mentioned models to make strategic decisions that set the course of the organization, decisions on what tactic to deploy to get the work done, and decisions made for the day-to-day operation of the organization.

Recognizing Biases in Decision Making

Biases are an integral part of human consciousness and may significantly affect business decisions, leading to less optimal conditions or even missing opportunities. Therefore, the identification and mitigation of these predispositions are important for improving the quality of decisions and increasing the chances of business success. Here are typical biases that happen very often in decision-making:

- **Groupthink Bias**: Entrepreneurs would either be under social stress or would just go with the flow of action by peers or competitors without critically analyzing their decisions. The subjection of the entrepreneur to group behavior may lead to emulation rather than thinking out of the box and, finally, to homogeneity and lost opportunities for innovation and development.

- **Sunk Cost Bias**: Entrepreneurs, at times, continue to plow resources (e.g., time, money, and effort) into a losing venture or project, especially if they have invested so much in the endeavor. This bias makes one ignore the issue of opportunity cost and can result in losses spiraling into bigger losses. The areas where this is a bit particular for the entrepreneur to throw in the towel are shown below.

- **Confirmation Bias**: Entrepreneurs have a tendency to look for evidence that confirms concepts or assumptions they have already formed while refuting evidence is mostly ignored. With this bias, there is a possibility of getting stuck with favored approaches or even disregarding alternative views. Because of this bias, entrepreneurs may find themselves attached to strategies that are no longer serving them or the team they belong to.

- **Overconfidence Bias**: Entrepreneurs sometimes exhibit unbridled confidence in their abilities, judgments, or the venture they have taken. Such excessive confidence sometimes leads them to extreme risk acceptance, regardless of prospective risks and undervaluing competition. This, as a result, can totally miss the emerging market shifts that will take place and not be able to recognize any looming threats on the horizon.

- **Anchoring Bias**: Occurs when people give more weight to initial pieces of information or reference points when they are making their choices. Business owners may dwell on a single factor, such as past performance or industry norms, and block out new information. In most cases, entrepreneurs who are emotionally engaged with or even under pressure to act immediately with a situation are likely to become prey to this bias as well. This could, however, sometimes be a problem since the information available may occasionally be incomplete, causing wrong decisions.

- **Availability Bias:** This bias arises from the tendency to overestimate information that is readily available or easily recalled. Business owners might disproportionately focus on current events or extreme cases when risk assumptions are changed. For example, an organization that is the victim of a cyber-attack could be seen to imply that a lot more money will be spent on preventing a replay from happening than on other very important concerns, which aren't as high profile but are significant.

Ways to Recognize Bias

Enhanced Awareness: Entrepreneurs can be aware of their typical tendencies if they are educated about cognitive psychology and the science of decision-making. The very awareness that biases exist is the first step toward lessening their effects.

- **Decision Audits**: Regular audits of decisions made and their outcomes reveal them as an eventual pattern of bias or errors in judgment. Entrepreneurs have the opportunity to realize instances in which the decisions taken are being influenced by biases and make the necessary corrections to enable them to make better decisions in the future.

- **Encourage diverse perspectives**: Enticing contrasting opinions and welcoming critical analysis of decisions can help in ceasing the confirmation bias and inculcate broader thinking in your decisions. Sometimes, playing a champion's role rather than a leader brings out deeply ingrained perspectives and urges others to entertain them, which is very beneficial for an entrepreneur not to have just an echo chamber around him. Make certain that your organization possesses a cocktail of varied perspectives for improved decision-making and betterment.

- **Making Use of Decision-Making Tools**: Various tools for decision-making, including decision trees, scenario planning, and SWOT analysis, provide logical formats in which one can check the alternatives and threats. With reasoned thought on the available alternatives and considerations on a vast array of scenarios, business owners are able to reduce the impact of bias on their deciding process.

- **Looking for Diverse Inputs**: Dealing with diverse people can give multiple perspectives, cutting down the effects of groupthink. This could be due to input being obtained from people with different backgrounds and experiences.

Entrepreneurs can therefore learn about hidden areas in one's processes in making predispositions.

Tools for Informed Decision Making

Apart from telling the structures of decision-making and giving indications of predispositions, entrepreneurs may use various tools and techniques to make well-informed and assisted decisions. These tools offer organized strategies for evaluating choices, examining threats, and examining possible end results, thus improving the chances of effective decision outcomes.

Decision Trees

Decision trees are visual representations of decision-making processes, highlighting numerous choices, their potential outcomes, and the possibilities related to each result. Entrepreneurs can use decision trees to methodically assess choices, recognize crucial choice factors, and evaluate the anticipated value of various selections.

How to apply

a. Determine important decision options within the decision-making process and write them out using nodes.

b. Evaluate the outcome of multiple results or occasions related to each decision.

c. Determine Expected Value: Multiply the possibility of each result by its matching reward or energy to compute the predicted outcome of each option.

d. Select the option with the greatest anticipated value or energy based on the decision tree evaluation.

Let's say that an entrepreneur is considering purchasing a brand-new product. Using a decision tree, they analyze the connected benefits (earnings or losses) based on marketing problems and customer needs. By measuring the possibilities and benefits, the business owner can figure out the optimum financial investment technique that makes the best use of anticipated value.

SWOT Analysis

SWOT analysis is a critical preparation tool used to examine a company's strengths, weaknesses, opportunities, and threats. By methodically assessing internal abilities and external factors, business owners can recognize crucial calculated problems, prioritize campaigns, and develop action plans to capitalize on strengths and minimize weaknesses.

How to apply

a. Identify the internal variables that add to the company's affordable benefit (e.g., special capacities, sources, or abilities) and areas for improvement or vulnerability.

b. Evaluate the external business environment, which consists of market patterns, affordable features, and prevailing changes that provide opportunities for development or present risks to the company.

c. Based on the SWOT analysis, existing approaches to utilizing strengths, addressing weaknesses, leveraging opportunities, and eliminating threats must align with the company's objectives and purposes.

Let's assume that an entrepreneur is preparing to get into a brand-new market and performs a SWOT analysis to examine the advantages as well as risks connected with the development. By assessing internal strengths (e.g., technical know-how) and weaknesses (e.g., limited brand identity) together with external opportunities (e.g., expanding need for cutting-edge items) and threats (e.g., extreme competitors), the business owner can create a market entry strategy that makes use of its strengths while minimizing possible risks.

Cost-Benefit Analysis

Cost-benefit analysis is a methodical strategy for reviewing the costs and benefits of different strategies to establish one of the most cost-effective options. By measuring both substantial and intangible costs and benefits, business owners can examine the factors that influence their decisions and focus on financial investments or jobs that provide the best value.

How to apply

a. Enumerate all appropriate costs (e.g., future financial investments, operating budget) and benefits (e.g., profit generation, savings) related to each decision option.

b. Assign a financial value to abstract elements such as brand name credibility, consumer satisfaction, or ecological influence to help with comparison across choices.

c. Determine Net Present Value (NPV): Subtract future capital from its present value using an ideal discount rate. Then, determine the present value of each alternative by deducting overall costs from overall benefits.

d. Select the choice with the highest present value or the best benefit-cost proportion as the recommended decision.

Let's say that an entrepreneur is reviewing two financial investment jobs with various capital forecasts as well as financial investment needs. By carrying out a cost-benefit analysis and comparing the present value of the jobs, the business owner can establish which financial investment possibility provides the greatest ROI and aligns with the company's calculated goals.

Scenario Planning

Scenario planning is a decision-making process that includes establishing several probable future circumstances to prepare for and a plan for uncertainties. By discovering different prospects and their possible implications, business owners can determine very early caution signals to adjust to transforming situations and minimize dangers related to unforeseen occasions.

How to apply

a. Identify essential variables or unclear variables that may substantially affect the business environment or sector.

b. Generate numerous situations that stand for various possible results for the determined unpredictability.

c. Analyze the possible ramifications of each circumstance on the company's approach, processes, and cost-efficient position.

d. Develop versatile methods and backup strategies that enable the company to respond properly to various future situations and maximize arising possibilities.

For example, an entrepreneur operating in the automobile sector prepares for technical interruption from independent cars and trucks as well as electrical flexibility. By establishing situations that discover various fostering prices, governing settings, and customer choices, the business owner can proactively change the business's item offerings, supply chain, and service design to continue to be affordable in a quickly advancing market.

Overcoming Decision-Making Paralysis

Decision-making is an essential element of entrepreneurship. Whether it's selecting between advertising methods, employing choices, or financial investment possibilities, business owners frequently encounter options that can dramatically influence the trajectory of their endeavors. Nonetheless, the process of decision-making isn't constantly simple; it can be stuffed with obstacles like decision fatigue as well as evaluation paralysis, which can prevent development as well as bring about missed out on opportunities.

Decision fatigue is described as a wearing-down effect of high-quality decisions one would make following a prolonged process of making decisions. Very much like physical fatigue, decision fatigue may render decisions complex as the day progresses. This is most problematic in a business environment with continuous decision-making, and most cases are high-stake options.

On the other hand, decision paralysis is a state of indecision that the myriad of presented choices puts an individual in. In today's fast-paced business world, most people are literally overwhelmed by information and, at the same time, by the importance of the decision that must be made. This is exactly why, in the fast-paced business world of today, a business owner can be paralyzed into making the wrong choice.

Strategies to Overcome Decision Paralysis

There are a number of ways in which business owners can manage decision-making paralysis. My personal favorite tool to overcome decision paralysis is the Eisenhower Matrix. The Eisenhower Matrix was first proposed by President Dwight D. Eisenhower and later popularized by Stephen Covey. There, you can categorize tasks into four quadrants based on their importance and urgency. Then, you can take action based on the task position. By doing so, you can focus more on the task that really matters and reduce the overwhelm you feel. Here are some tips to overcome decision paralysis you can use along with the Eisenhower Matrix:

1. **Establish Decision-Making Criteria**: Undoubtedly, setting the standards for making a decision can properly provide the necessary structure in reviewing the alternatives and proceeding with the choice, which is well informed, whether in reviewing the potential threats, the consideration of the economic impact, or ensuring that the selected alternatives would be chosen within the long-run goals. Predetermined criteria can increase the quality of the decisions and also reduce variation.

2. **Focus on Choices**: Not all decisions are equal; by focusing on the importance and urgency dimensions in making decisions, the business owner can economize on their time and resources. Tools such as the Eisenhower Matrix help a business owner hold his or her attention to only those activities that really count.

3. **Delegate decisions**: The entrepreneur does not have to make all of the decisions single-handedly. Delegating decisions to reliable staff members who have appropriate knowledge can lighten the load and guarantee that choices are made within their areas of duty, which not only eases the business owner of decision fatigue but also cultivates a feeling of freedom and responsibility within the group.

4. **Action-Oriented Mindset**: Along with utilizing particular methods, growing an action-oriented attitude is important for conquering decision-making paralysis. This state of mind is defined by prejudice in the direction of activity where insufficient choices are chosen due to unpredictability. Rather than making every effort for excellence, business owners must concentrate on making progress and picking up from their blunders along the road. By accepting a culture of trials and plans, business owners can eliminate the fear of failure and move their endeavors ahead.

Growing a Decision-Making Culture

While specific decision-making is crucial, growing a decision-making culture within a team can magnify the solid decision-making culture defined by open interaction, approval, and a common dedication to quality. A decision-making culture is necessary for a number of factors:

- **Promotes Collaboration**: When staff members feel encouraged to articulate their points of view and contribute to the decision-making process, it promotes collaboration and harmony within the group. By leveraging its participants' varied points of view and experience, the team can come to even more innovative and efficient options.

- **Promotes Accountability**: In a team where decision-making is clear and comprehensive, staff members are most likely to take ownership of their decisions and be answerable for their outcomes. This fosters a feeling of obligation and drives continual transformation within the company.

- **Drives Innovation**: A decision-making culture fosters innovation and business growth by encouraging trying something new and taking risks. An innovation culture that drives business growth is born when employees perceive the power to try something original and test the status quo.

Relevance of Interaction and Open-Door Policies

Consistent communication is fundamental to a strong decision-making culture. To develop open dialogue and facilitate productive decision-making, entrepreneurs can try to implement the following practices:

- **Encourage Openness**: Establish a supporting atmosphere in which employees genuinely feel at ease and can express their opinions, even in opposition to the prevailing attitudes, and question their existing knowledge. Entrepreneurs need to participate in a number of opinion presentations and brainstorming exercises to lead creativity and collaboration better.

- **Seek Diverse Perspectives**: Now, there is an availability of employees or team members with a different background, experiences, and varied decision-making processes in order to get meaningful insights.

- **Provide Constructive Feedback**: Develop a culture of feedback in which workers have the power to speak up with applicable objections and help others overall. If feedback is usefully given constructively, then the group understands and moves on.

- **Delegating Authority**: Delegating authority can be considered the process that permits the staff to make decisions of their own free will within their areas of competence. This activity is vital in developing high trust in people and taking up ownership of the job. It can only make the staff feel that the job belongs to them, and it is about the responsibility that propels the business to the next step.

- **Clarify Roles and Responsibilities**: I pointed out the need to clarify what every staff member does in the office to ensure clarity and accountability. Clear expectations from the beginning empower an owner to empower employees, then make decisions on their own and give meaning to business objectives.

- **Provide Training and Support**: Organize training programs with clear guidelines so that staff may acquire newly imparted skills and knowledge. This will aid in situating them for better decision-making. Business owners must help staff in the development process through consistent support and coaching to facilitate growth in their places of work.

- **Observe Successes and Learn from Failures**: Recognize and celebrate successes to condition acceptable behaviors and motivate employees. It may also help a culture for resilience—

one in which it celebrates failure as learning toward growing and becoming better.

- **Keeping Transparency with Stakeholders**: A business owner should be open and candid in all his business dealings with investors, customers, employees, business partners, and regulators. This may even involve the business owner making public disclosures relevant to the discernment of modalities related to business operations, the financial performance of the business, its ecological impact, and the culture within.

- **Ensuring Fair Treatment of Employees**: Entrepreneurs, in any way, should be fair with all the staff and other employees, providing reasonable salaries, secure working conditions, and professional development. In several cases, this could result in demanding decisions like hiring and even firing while trying to remain fair and just.

- **Firmness**: Firmness is an absolute requirement. Business people need to exercise a strong moral fiber in the face of tough decisions. It calls for this if one is to persist with being courageous, honest, and committed to what is right, especially when it could be far more tempting to give up beliefs in the interest of self-profit.

- **Lead by Example**: An entrepreneur should show exemplary leadership through example and an honest attitude toward others. Business owners will get much loyalty not only from the people under their employ but also from consumers and other stakeholders when they lead by example with firmness and openness.

- **Implement Ethical Codes of Conduct**: Clear standards or codes of ethics will guide decisions. Besides, it will bring uniformity and justice to your organization. The business owners may clearly communicate the belief system in the organization regarding what is considered permissible and what is not; this will guide the juniors in the decision-making process.

- **Accountability of Entrepreneurs**: Entrepreneur accountability is defined as the ability to take responsibility for personal and corporate actions. This may involve the installation of whistleblower mechanisms about the reporting of misdeeds, regular audits and studies, and proper punishment of behaviors suspected to have violated the entity's code of conduct.

Assessing Stakeholder Impact in Decision-Making

Business owners now have to make decisions considering how they may affect workers, clients, communities, and the environment. This is a concept that has heated up further over the decade as the world moves in slow steps toward taking on social impact and ESG considerations. In this connection, the business owners can have an intuitive feel of both the general level of contention and the maximum positive impact that is generated for all key stakeholders, including:

- **Carrying out Stakeholder Analysis**: In arriving at the final decision, the businessperson first considers what effects the decision is likely to have on other stakeholders. Businesses are therefore called upon to identify who the critical stakeholders are, analyze their interests and concerns, and investigate the possible implications of alternative courses of action.

- **Seeking Input and Feedback**: Stakeholders may bring to the table several ideas and points of view, which may not be so apparent at first. Important decisions are made concerning diverse stakeholders, who often carry an assortment of experiences and perceptions gained in the journey of life to ensure that such business owners make decisions that will be a reflection of the needs and priorities of those affected by them.

- **Minimizing Harm and Maximizing Benefits**: In any case of conflict, the business owner should try to minimize the level of harm and guarantee the situation being considered now brings the maximum benefit for all the stakeholders. This may include satisfying the stakeholder's level of interest and simultaneously including some precautionary measures so that care is taken for harmful consequences of the decision.

CHAPTER 4:
Building Resilience

As you explored the art form of decision-making, you discovered a better balance between rational analysis and intuition to help work through tough decisions involved in entrepreneurship; you learn how to identify and temper cognitive bias, become familiar with other ways of thinking about decision-making, and build your capacity for making solid and confident decisions. These are skills crucial for navigating your entrepreneurial path, but even the most well-reasoned choices sometimes feel like the wrong path when one is faced with blind alleys and missteps.

Moving right along to Chapter 4, we dive into another crucial quality: just that ability to bounce back and keep going when things get complicated. This chapter is meant to guide you to take inherent challenges and turn them into areas of growth and innovation. You will also learn about the psychological underpinnings of resilience and learn some efficient strategies for developing it within yourself and your team. By developing resilience, you'll be better equipped to maintain motivation, adjust to constantly changing situations, and keep moving toward your goals—no matter how stormy the journey may get.

The meaning of resilience in entrepreneurship can be portrayed as the capacity to recapture from challenges and disappointments, to maintain proper motivation, and an energetic determination toward the achievement of a set goal. Resilience is, therefore, a dynamic process of awareness, development, and adaptation in the face of the world as a response to misfortune. Therefore, it is not being demanding or endurance but as opposed to how failure could be perceived as an opportunity rather than just a loss.

Significance of Resilience for Success

Resilience makes all the difference among entrepreneurs, and for good reasons. First, the entrepreneurship sector is flooded with uncertainties. Many challenges and risks of failing characterize it. Consequently, an ability to bounce back and move on despite the difficulties breeds the capability to advance toward achieving long-term goals.

In addition, resilience is an attribute that lets small business people remain steadfast and encouraged despite adverse events. Entrepreneurship has so many barriers, rejections, and objections that it becomes, in fact, an effective turnoff for people. It is the phenomenon in which resilience infuses into business owners positive expectations towards problems, dedication towards their vision, and ways to navigate ending up at successful solutions or anticipated states.

Most importantly, it adds to innovation and creativity for that individual. Resilient business owners are the most open to trying things out and taking rational risks, and they remain latched to no typical solutions to problems. These challenges are not taken by the entrepreneurs at face value; instead, they use them to learn and understand how things can be done differently in the future.

Mental Aspects of Resilience

Frameworks that dovetail psychological concepts can bring out exciting inferences into the nature of resilience and all that contributes to it. Similarly, the idea of resilience is that an individual has essential resilience and resources that allow adjustment in an efficient way against misfortune. It insists more on the variables, which include self-efficacy, positive outlook, and social support, in the promotion of resilience. On the other hand, positive psychology looks at how this acquired toughness is through resources helpful to mental health, in which mindset and emotional intelligence are crucial to understanding how people can build resilience through difficult experiences.

Factors Influencing Individual Resilience

There are a veritable number of factors that influence individual differences in resilience. One appears to be a factor relating to outlook, whereby failure builds either a fixed or a growth mindset. Adversity is looked at by people with a growth mindset as something passing and huge for an opportunity to learn and grow from. On the other hand, a fixed mindset will most likely look at failure as an indication that one is fundamentally, by nature, inefficient and thus fundamentally inefficient; this could induce feelings of helplessness and hopelessness.

Besides social support, personality characteristics also play another role in resilience, whereby optimism, persistence, and openness will affect an individual's resilience to thrive. Applying a more excellent, optimistic, hopeful disposition gives rise to many positive expectations of the best under the worst adversities. The more persistent person will keep on with vigor and pursue the goals. One who is open to new experiences in life is, of course, flexible and will consider new alternatives in the face of dire odds.

These adaptive strategies serve to augment resilience. Suitable coping methods such as problem resolution, social support, and turning negative thoughts into positive ones help to manage stress, anxiety, and adversity. When business owners exhaust resourceful coping techniques, they remain more robust against rough times, thus transitioning through turbulent periods with much ease.

Why Do Individuals Struggle to Be Resilient?

Although resilience is important, not many people can develop this essential quality. Resilience is best developed over time. Several factors cause the problem of building the resilience people have:

1. **Fear of Failure**: It can prevent one from taking risks or even pervade the dread of trying to accomplish something. This is in fact based on a social assumption, perfectionism, and a fixed mindset that perceives failure as equivalent to total inadequacy.

Overcoming this anxiety will require the definition of failure as an ordinary and inevitable part of learning—and a place for growth.

2. **Absence of Self-efficacy**: One of the most vital components of resilience is self-efficacy, the belief in oneself to perform a task. On the contrary, low self-efficacy makes one doubt one's abilities, and one faces problems while bouncing back from the issues. Fostering self-efficacy requires setting attainable goals, learning the skills and competence that are needed, and seeking mentors from both seniors and colleagues who are encouraging.

3. **Limited Social Support**: Social support is any such thing that protects against stress and disaster—it builds resilience in times of adversity. Persons with no sound, solid support will find it hard to work through problems when issues arise. Making an affirming set of advisors, peers, and professionals can appropriate support and aid during hard times.

4. **Negative Thinking Patterns**: They are such as catastrophizing, over generalizing, and personalizing, lower resilience by magnifying impacts when one is faced with challenges and chipping away at one's positive self-image. Being cogently behaviorally orientated, cognitive restructuring and mindfulness are some of how the rethinking and re-election of negative ideas are approached in a move to foster resilience in the state of mind.

Creating a Resilience Mindset

In my experience working as an entrepreneur, creating a resilience mindset is easier said than done. However, this is achievable. I believe some basics that aid an entrepreneur in managing the lows and highs of business effectively are a more positive attitude, persistence, adaptability, mindfulness, and self-awareness. These mindsets have supported me throughout my journey.

1. **Positive Outlook**: They say optimism is the frame through which resilience can flourish. This is the empowering view that business owners should hold at times of challenge and barrier. An optimistic business owner will view every stumbling block as an open door to realizing their strength. Obstacles—those temporary challenges on the path to success—are viewed as opportunities by the business owner. In his view, opportunities come as a result of obstacles. Optimistic business owners will manage to extract positive experiences through an adverse event, hence maintaining the drive and strength to pursue the goal.

2. **Determination**: Perseverance is the ability to persist despite challenges and problems. Promising entrepreneurs have a clear understanding that failure is not the end but rather a stepping stone towards success. They practice resiliency by sticking with their passion in the face of adversity or rejection. In internalizing a growth mindset and seeing challenges as areas to grow,

entrepreneurs can have that doggedness to fight off obstacles and ultimately pursue their dreams.

3. **Adaptability**: It means accepting the uncertainty that welcomes changing circumstances. It is in every occurrence of change that takes place, and in entrepreneurship, good business people should be those who should welcome these changes with open arms quickly in new situations and marketing conditions. An entrepreneur can confidently wade through the sea of uncertainty to turn hindrances into possibilities for further growth and development by being adaptive and open to new things. It helps the entrepreneur to be at his ultimate best since he is adaptive to rapid occurrences that take place during uncertain times.

4. **Mindfulness and Self-Awareness**: Mindfulness strategies, including meditation and other mindfulness exercises, would help entrepreneurs develop self-awareness and emotional toughness. By exercising mindfulness, business owners can develop a much deeper understanding of their thoughts, feelings, and responses to stress factors. This self-awareness allows them to acknowledge when they are really feeling overwhelmed or distressed and take proactive action to handle their anxiety as well as keep their cool.

Structure Resilience in Teams

While individual strength is essential, building resilience within business teams is similarly essential for lasting success. Right here are some methods for cultivating a society of durability within groups:

- **Cultivating a Culture of Resilience**: Building an empowering workplace where team members really feel valued, appreciated, and motivated to take risks or bounce back from failure. Leaders can establish the tone by modeling resilience and providing opportunities for employees to build their resilience while participating in professional training and development programs. By cultivating a culture of resilience, groups can much better navigate obstacles and provide support to each other, becoming more powerful and also a lot more skilled as an outcome.

- **Interaction Strategies**: Effective interaction is necessary for building team resilience. Encouraging open and honest interaction, active listening, and positive responses can help staff members to really feel listened to and seen, promoting a feeling of being trusted and a partnership within the group. In times of crisis or uncertainty, clear interaction about difficulties, goals, and strategies can help minimize anxiety and develop resilience by cultivating a common feeling of function and unity.

- **Leveraging Diversity and Collaboration**: Diversity in viewpoints, backgrounds, and experiences can be an effective asset for developing resilience in groups. By welcoming variety and building a culture of inclusivity, teams can take advantage of differences in viewpoints and strategies for analyzing situations, boosting their capacity to adjust and restrategize when faced with difficulty. Partnership and team efforts are likewise important for building resilience, as they allow employees to sustain and rely upon each other throughout the bumpy rides of corporate jobs. By leveraging the strength of each staff member and collaborating in the direction of common objectives, groups can conquer barriers and emerge more powerful than in the past.

CHAPTER 5:

Effective Goal Setting

That's great that you learned about the essence of resilience in entrepreneurship: how to turn failures into stepping stones and how to keep yourself on a driven and motivated track when something goes wrong. You looked at the underpinnings of resilience from a psychological point of view and discovered helpful ways of developing and preserving this key characteristic within you and your team. So, with the shield of resilience, you are ready now to charge headlong into challenges and turn stumbling blocks into stepping stones.

Ahead lay the art and science of practical goal setting—a process that takes your visions and dreams and renders them into achievable milestones. As we travel through this chapter, you shall learn how to set goals that inspire and drive tangible progress and success. You will learn why your goals need to be SMART-specific, Measurable, Achievable, Relevant, and Time-bound and how this pertains to personal well-being and business goals. The chapter further equips you with practical tools on how to build an effective action plan and stay focused so that your goals are no longer a wish but are achievable milestones towards your entrepreneurial journey.

I will start by giving you two distinct scenarios. First up is Maya, a young, beautiful, and passionate entrepreneur who has just started her journey in the technology industry. She believes that technology has great potential to change the lives of people and has a desire to impact her world. Maya decided to create both a website and a mobile app that connects farmers with their direct consumers. She believes this will help both the farmers and consumers and cut out middlemen and the disadvantages of middlemen. So Maya set SMART (specific, measurable, achievable, relevant, and time-bound) goals and wrote out action plans to achieve them (that is, both the website and the mobile app). After three months of hard work and sleepless nights, everything was ready, and it was launched.

She got a good number of users and investors too, and as the user base increased, she set higher goals to help scale more and maintain balance.

The next is Tom, another technology enthusiast, and a passionate entrepreneur. He identified that a productivity app could help a lot of people out. He was so excited about his discovery and, with the sugar rush to bring this to life, that he dove into developing the app without a clear picture of what he wanted to achieve and without setting clear and strategic goals. This took a stressful turn on the team because each day, he came up with new changes to the app. The team members kept working on several features that most likely could be trashed the next day because "Tom has a new idea". Several months passed by, and the app never came to life, which weighed everyone on the team down. Some team members even left the team.

What is the difference between these two scenarios? *SMART Goals and Action Plans.*

"Setting goals is the first step in turning the invisible into the visible." - Tony Robbins. Tony Robbins was not telling a lie when he made that statement. I have listened to a lot of people speak about their journey to success, and one thing I find common among all of them is that they had to identify what they wanted to achieve, set clear goals, and then take action to bring their dreams to life. Goals turn an individual's dreams, desires, or ambitions into tangible results. It gives one clarity and a sense of direction as to what steps they need to take to turn their desires into reality. Goal setting is the process of defining the target that you, as an entrepreneur, aim to achieve. It involves identifying the target and strategically developing plans to help one hit the target.

Every entrepreneur should think about where the business is currently and where they would like it to be. It is ideal for an entrepreneur to create a picture of where he or she wants the business to be. Although it is not always possible to achieve the ideal picture, they can effectively set goals that can turn these pictures into a reality. As an entrepreneur with the ambition to thrive and not just survive in a world full of competition, effective goal setting will motivate not just the individual but also their team, provide a sense of direction, and serve as a roadmap to their destination. Effective goal-setting will transform one's ambitions and dreams into reality.

Note that effective goal setting is an important skill. In developing this skill, one has to carefully and intentionally take into consideration where their business is currently and where they want it to be and strategically set goals that can help them to achieve success. It is a skill one must possess as an entrepreneur if you want to succeed. Let's delve more into the topic of effective goal setting.

Why Do People Fail to Set Goals?

Anxiety

Among all the reasons that prevent people from setting goals, the most common is the fear of fraud. Goals set us up to get out of our comfort zone and take risks. Yet, this fear can also be disabling, making us avoid setting any. Many folks are scared stiff that they might be tagged as incompetent or worse if a goal is not attained after being set. As a result, they may avoid setting goals entirely to save themselves from ever feeling pain from failure.

One human fear that is rationed is the fear of failure. Failing can be said to be a matter of survival. Our beings are wired so that the possibility of failing is the last-resort mechanism, making it very hard for human beings to take risks while striving to work their way up in life.

Yet, at the same time, it is this fear that will, in yet other ways, hold us back from achieving our potential. So, in the shadows of our fears, we will be allowed opportunities for success to waste away because time waits for no person. Rather than taking risks and venturing out of our comfort zones, we live a mediocre lifestyle and remain within our safe circle.

Lack of Confidence

One of the most common reasons many people have difficulty setting their goals is due to self-doubt in achieving them. They might question whether they have what it requires to attain their objectives and might be afraid that they will certainly not have the ability to manage the difficulties as well as barriers along the road. This uncertainty can stop them from establishing ambitious goals and choosing mediocrity instead.

The lack of self-confidence is usually rooted in low self-confidence might tell themselves that they are not good enough, clever enough, or skilled enough to accomplish their objectives. They might compare themselves to others and come up with the conclusion that they will certainly never ever measure up.

Nonetheless, self-confidence is not something that you either have or you do not have. It is an ability that can be developed in time with technique and determination. By challenging negative self-talk, establishing small, achievable objectives, and commemorating your successes along the road, you can build your self-confidence and handle larger obstacles.

Lack of Clarity

Most people have difficulty developing their goals simply because they do not have a clear idea about what they want to achieve. At best, they have some general notion about what they would like, but they don't identify their desires and the paths they must take to reach them. People cannot develop meaningful and attainable goals if they do not know what they want to accomplish.

Without a clear purpose, one is likely to feel lost and directionless. Without some clear purpose or intent of knowing what they want, it is pretty easy to drift from job to job, doing things. This will stack a person with stress, unhappiness, and fatigue.

Try to find your goals and what you want to achieve. What are the most critical things or things you can do, and what do you succeed in your life? Break down the goals into small and achievable pieces and then formulate a plan on how to do so.

Fear of Success

This fear of success is sometimes equally limiting, as many people are afraid that success would mean having to handle increased responsibility, stress, and expectations. That is how people sometimes sabotage themselves, whether consciously or subconsciously, or avoid trying to set high goals to prevent the pain of succeeding. Then again, fear of success is an absolute oxymoron because, after all, isn't it what most people want to achieve in this lifetime? True, but sometimes success can be so overpowering. It changes our lives in ways that we perhaps might not entirely be ready for, let alone the fact that it brings with it new challenges on top of responsibilities. One needs to understand that success is not a destination but a journey. This is not an achievement at one point but an evolving process of learning and, over time, developing a better version of one. The process of growth and development takes years, and making it in life comes from within, not being laser-focused on getting the end result and overcoming the fear of success.

Perfectionism

Yet, goal setting is the first step. Of course, perfectionism throws many blocks up to setting a goal. Sometimes, we set the bar so high that it seems almost pointless even to make the goal unless we are sure to reach it. There may be a fear that if one should set a goal and not quite achieve it, then one would be looked at as a failure. So, perhaps one would not set any goals, or we'd put them so low that little motivation or challenge is involved.

Either perfectionism can be a two-edged sword. This is our ticket to great things and, in a way, a driver to push ourselves to be the best we can be. On the other hand, it can hold us back from taking risks and pursuing our goals for fear of not being able to meet our own incredibly high standards.

To overcome perfectionism, it is essential to acknowledge that no one is perfect. Most of us make errors and fail to achieve our goals once in a while. What is necessary is that we learn from our blunders, readjust our strategy as required, and forge ahead. By focusing on progress, as opposed to excellence, we can conquer our anxiety of failing and attain our goals.

Overwhelm

In today's fast-paced world, many individuals really feel bewildered by the large variety of goals they might establish. They might have a lot of competing priorities and obligations that they do not understand where to begin. Consequently, they might stall or stay clear of establishing objectives entirely, causing an absence of direction and purpose.

Feeling overwhelmed can be immobilizing. We feel like we're drowning in an ocean of responsibilities. It leads to anxious, tense feelings, and exhaustion. To get rid of being overwhelmed, listen for your goals and concentrate your attention on the things that matter to you. Start with what your significant priorities are and then break those down into more specific objectives. Then, get ready to pursue it verb by verb, starting with the most important.

Lack of Accountability

After all, goal setting typically tends to be somewhat challenging for many based on a lack of accountability. That is because the individual has a vague perception of what it is that they may want to achieve, but without a concrete plan and motivation towards achieving some of their goals, it is all too easy to procrastinate and allow one to fall further and further from staying on course. Accountability toward the fulfillment of one's goals inherently helps a given individual to remain resilient and focused.

One of the things that make goal-setting work is accountability. If you know people are watching and they will hold you accountable for what you do or don't do, then there is more oomph to keep motivated and focused on your goal. That is why a set-in-place support system of this kind is so critically important.

To go about this, find someone to hold you accountable. He or she could be a friend, family member, mentor, or teacher to whom you trust. Share with them what you're working on and see if they wouldn't mind taking a keen interest in following up and checking in on how you're doing about that work. The knowledge that somebody is watching and holding your feet close to the fire will go a long way to help you achieve those goals.

What Are SMART Goals?

SMART goals provide a practical guideline for setting practical goals. SMART is an acronym for Specific, Measurable, Achievable, Relevant, and Time-bound goals. Setting SMART goals gives you a clear picture of what you want to achieve and the time frame within which this goal is to be achieved. Also, it helps you track your progress. Let's look more into the acronym "SMART".

S - Specific

Imagine driving on a road with many routes but not knowing which one leads to your destination. This is like having ambitions without clear goals. In setting effective goals, clarity is key; clearly specify your goal. Let it be well-defined, not vague. Your goals should be specific and consistent with your business's mission and vision. Examples of specific goals are "decrease the cost of generation by making way better deals with the suppliers" rather than "decrease the cost of generation", "increase the number of product users to 100 users" rather than "increase the number of product users", etc. Specific goals help you understand the objective and also eliminate distractions because you have a clear picture of what you aim to achieve.

M - Measurable

Let your goal be quantifiable. This makes it easy for you to track your progress and review your action plans to make the necessary adjustments. Using milestones here would be helpful as this will help you know how far you have gone in your journey to success. While setting the goal, include the amount, period, etc. When your goals are measurable, it fosters accountability and makes the process more exciting. Who would not be happy to see that they are making progress with their goals? Here are some examples of measurable goals; "Increase the number of product users to 1000 users in 3 months", "decrease the cost of generation by 20% by arranging way better deals with the suppliers", etc.

A - Achievable

Of course, it is good to be optimistic when setting goals, but be honest with yourself while setting your goals. Set goals that are realistic and achievable. Keep it real. Take into consideration your capabilities, things that may limit you, the given period, resources, and circumstances. Some people misunderstand the idea of thinking big and tend to set unrealistic goals, and when they fail to achieve this, their confidence and self-esteem are affected. Sometimes, they even feel like failures. So, set realistic goals. Setting realistic goals does not mean in any way that you should set goals that are too easy. Now, imagine an entrepreneur who owns an e-commerce site and has a goal to increase their monthly site traffic by 30% within six months. To attain this, they use digital marketing strategies like SEO optimization, influencers, and social media publicity to increase their traffic. They make adjustments to their strategies where necessary and implement the use of analytic tools to track their progress. After six months, the traffic on their site has increased by 33%. This was an achievable goal, it was specific and measurable, and also the right strategies and actions were taken. An example of an unachievable goal would be an entrepreneur who lacks experience in the food industry and just starts a restaurant to be the top restaurant in 3 months in a street that has six restaurants already, just because they are "thinking big". Yes, the goal is specific and measurable, but it is unachievable.

R - Relevant

Relevant goals are goals that align with your business's mission, vision, and values. The question here is, why are you setting this goal? How will achieving this goal impact the business? Setting relevant goals helps you focus on the bigger picture. Irrelevant goals are a waste of time. Remember the first scenario from our previous point: the entrepreneur who runs an e-commerce site and wants to increase the traffic on the site by 30% within six months and takes the necessary steps to get this done. That is a relevant goal because by increasing their traffic, their business grows. An example of an irrelevant goal would be an entrepreneur who owns a restaurant but sets a goal to learn how to play piano within three months. That is a good goal, but it is a personal goal and is not relevant to the growth of your business.

T - Time-Bound

When a goal is time-bound, it has a timeframe or deadline for completion. Time-bound goals help you focus on the target and keep you on your toes. When your goals are not time-bound, you tend to procrastinate, which causes a delay in the completion of the goal. The more the goal completion is prolonged, the more you lose the drive to achieve or complete the goal. For example, an entrepreneur wants to increase the traffic on their site by 30% within six months. A specific number of months has been set. Time is allocated to implement the digital marketing strategies and review their progress. Imagine an entrepreneur's goal is to 'grow their restaurant into a luxurious one'. That is a nice goal, but it is not time-bound.

Example of SMART Goals

Here are comprehensive examples of SMART goals that can serve as a guide:

Increase monthly traffic on the website by 30%:
- *Specific*: Increase the monthly number of page views from 120 to 156 and the conversion rate from 45% to 59%

- *Measurable*: The increase in traffic on the website can be easily measured using analytical tools.

- *Achievable*: The use of strategic marketing can help achieve this goal.

- *Relevant*: It is relevant to the advancement of the business.

- *Time-Bound*: Achieve this within six months.

Boost business profit by 20%:

- *Specific*: Boost business profit from $100,000 to $120,000.

- *Measurable*: An increase in the monthly income can be measured.

- *Achievable*: This can be achieved through strategic marketing.

- *Relevant*: This goal is relevant to the growth of the business.

- *Time-Bound*: This goal is to be achieved in 4 months.

Boost the satisfaction of the product users to 70%:

- *Specific*: Boost the satisfaction of the product users 50% to 70%.

- *Measurable*: Survey exercises can be used to measure the progress of this goal.

- *Achievable*: This can be achieved by improving customer care services.

- *Relevant*: Increasing the satisfaction of the users increases the user base and the loyalty of the customers.

- *Time-Bound*: This goal is to be achieved in 4 months.

Decrease the cost of generation by 10 % in 7 months:
- *Specific*: Decrease the cost of generation by 10 % by making way better deals with the suppliers.

- *Measurable*: This can be measured by tracking the cost of generation every month.

- *Achievable*: This can be achieved by making way better deals with the suppliers.

- *Relevant*: This increases the business's income.

- *Time-Bound*: This goal is to be achieved in 10 months.

Benefits of Setting Smart Goals as an Entrepreneur

Setting SMART goals improves the overall productivity of the team and gives the entrepreneur and their team a clear focus on what they are to achieve and an action plan to work with to achieve this goal. They are able to identify their priorities and avoid distractions.

When entrepreneurs set SMART goals, they and their team stay motivated and committed, taking the necessary steps and putting in the effort and time required to achieve them. This gives them a sense of control, which in turn boosts their confidence.

Setting SMART goals helps entrepreneurs track their progress using milestones. This can help them know if they're moving forward or backward, review their progress, and make the necessary adjustments where needed. Knowing that they are making progress keeps them excited, and has the opportunity to celebrate when they achieve milestones. Also, being able to track their progress eliminates the waste of time on irrelevant activities.

By setting SMART goals, entrepreneurs get to set their priorities right and focus on achieving the goals. This helps the entrepreneur manage their time effectively and avoid distractions. This, in turn, helps them make better choices that are in line with their goals and the results they desire to achieve.

Setting SMART goals helps each team member know and understand the roles they need to play in contributing to the achievement of the goal and their responsibilities. Hence, they can be held accountable for tasks allocated to them. Accountability is advantageous in the sense that it makes room for easy adjustments and improvements to be made.

In the case where an entrepreneur is trying to deal with a challenge, setting SMART goals helps the entrepreneur have a detailed and structured plan to work with in order to arrive at the required solution. By doing this, they can allocate the necessary resources and employ proper strategies to solve the problem.

Setting SMART goals is important if you desire to succeed as an entrepreneur. Also, you derive a sense of satisfaction when you achieve your goals and attain success in your business.

Creating Your Action Plan

It is not enough to set SMART goals. I've seen several cases where a person set SMART goals but still failed to achieve them. This is where action plans come in. Alongside your goals should be your action plan. An action plan contains detailed and structured information on the tasks, steps, and out in order for your goals to be achieved. It is a roadmap for turning your goals into practical steps. An action plan takes the whole process and breaks it down into smaller bits based on the timeframe. Without an action plan, there's a high tendency of you taking your eyes off the target. You will most likely delay your progress and go into deeper realms of procrastination. On the other hand, the advantage of having an action plan is that it helps you stay focused, motivated, and committed to your course of success. It also makes tracking your progress and accountability easy. Let's take a look at how to write an action plan.

Once you are done writing out your SMART goals and have a clear picture and understanding of what you desire to achieve, the next thing to do is break these goals into small tasks. Each task should be linked together and all relevant to the achievement of your goals, just like the different compartments of a train, which are linked together and make up the whole train. Break the SMART goals into milestones, each milestone representing significant points in the achievement of your desired outcome. Once you have the milestones set, allocate timeframes to each milestone. The timeframe allocated to each milestone should be a breakdown of the overall time frame. So ensure that when you add the timeframe for each milestone, it does not exceed the timeframe for the goal. Next, take each milestone and break it down into smaller tasks using the SMART principle. Don't get confused; I'll give you a quick example. Let's say your big goal is to increase your social media presence by 30%; your milestones can be 10%, 20%, and then 30%. Now, to raise your online presence to 10%, by applying the SMART principle, your task could be to make two social media posts, one in the morning and the other in the evening, five days a week. You can proceed to set what time of day these posts will be made and what content you will post at various times.

After writing the tasks for the first milestone, proceed to do the same for the various milestones. Remember to use the SMART principle.

Next, you have to prioritize your tasks. Using the example above, say the five days you pick are from Monday to Friday; you cannot jump to Friday's tasks when you have not done Monday's tasks. There has to be orderliness. It's 10% first, before 20%, then 30%. Understand that not all tasks are of equal urgency or importance. The next thing to do is to delegate these tasks to various team members if you are working with a team. Who's going to handle the content creation for the post? Who's handling the social media post designs?

Who's in charge of managing the social media account? And so on. By doing this, each person knows what they're supposed to handle and when they are to deliver it. Don't forget to make the necessary resources required available. Also, create checkpoints. These are points where you review the work done so far and make the necessary adjustments where needed. Finally, always celebrate each milestone achieved, as this will boost your confidence and that of your team members.

Success is never an easy path or a miracle, but it is definitely achievable when you apply the right principles and take the right steps. By setting SMART goals, which serve as a roadmap in your journey of success, and creating an action plan to work with, you can effectively achieve your goals and attain great heights in the world of business.

CHAPTER 6:
The Power of Creative Thinking In Business

You came to know how the power of goal setting could translate your vision into reality and concrete actions. Most of your vision is now translated into SMART goals, and an action plan is built around it. Now, you have a well-structured road map of milestones that shall lead to success and make your entrepreneurial vision a reality.

Next, we will examine one of the most exciting topics of creativity and innovation. Indeed, creativity and innovation are things that an entrepreneur needs to be successful in business. Thus, in this chapter, you will learn how to make creativity a disciplined process rather than a random spark of brilliance, as you might harness continuous innovation. You will learn to create a culture that encourages innovation and, at the same time, discover ways to generate and implement new ideas that make your business unique in the competition. From product development and process optimization to business model innovation, this chapter shall instill in you the attitude and tools you need to become innovative and creative because continuous growth and success are established innovations.

As for innovation and creativity, entrepreneurship describes its accelerants in differentiation and development. They make you challenge the current approach so that you can imagine other possibilities to transform your unique imagination into actionable results. This chapter will show you techniques that will help you ignite creative thinking, overcome the most usual barriers to innovation, and mobilize your team's multiple perspectives into truly breakthrough solutions. Embracing creativity and innovation will not only make tremendous business sense but also make your journey of being a vibrant entrepreneur even more rewarding.

Creativity is the driving force that takes an organization's engine to novel areas of innovation and development. It does not only have to do with implementing innovations, but it breathes life into those ideas, converting them into tangible assets and adding value to the market. In this dynamic business environment, where competitors are struggling to attract interests and customers' preferences are changing like dunes in the wind, creativity surfaces to be the ace of trumps, the X-factor that lays one firm ahead of the others. It is this very power that animates the instinct for growth. It helps organizations to cross levels of adaptation.

Think of industry giants like Apple—a company practically synonymous with pioneering new products that marry cutting-edge technology with stylish design aesthetics. Or think, for that matter, of Nike—one of the biggest brand names in the world, but particularly in sport's shoes and apparel; it just keeps pushing the envelope with innovation through both its inspirational commercials and marketing and, of course, the design of new product offerings. Most of these industry titans owe most of their meteoric success to company cultures that never backed off the promotion of creativity at every turn.

Yet innovation is not limited to product development; it pervades every aspect of service operation, from marketing and advertising sponsorships to supply chain management. Companies like Amazon and Netflix demonstrate this fact, as they have reinvented entire industries through their purposely established processes of distribution and content delivery. With very potent creativity, services can only remain successful but set their course amidst the shifts of sands in market trends.

The Link Between Innovation and Creativity

Creative thinking and innovation are siblings, with the two relying on each other for existence and growth. In the scope of existence, creativity is the foundation upon which ideas are built, while innovation is the mechanism that changes naivety into productive uses. The absence of creativity, on the other hand, makes innovation monotonous, with practitioners in the synonymously related field having naught other than mere ideas and products.

From incremental improvements to processes and products that already exist in the market to revolutionary discoveries that alter the whole business landscape, innovations come in all sizes. At every step of this process of change, innovative thinking provides the guiding light that sheds luminescent brightness on the path ahead, and from the very onset, thinking instills the process of advancement with poignancy and objectiveness.

Creativity, on its own, is not enough and needs to be nurtured and developed in a corporate culture. Again, organizations that foster a culture of creativity permit their employees to think beyond what is usual, test the norm, and passionately look for new solutions. It is this culture of development that sets the platform to take off for innovation to soar high.

Difficulties in Unleashing Creativity

Indeed, entrepreneurs often come to battle with the ghostly specter of failure that waits just around the corner. The very prospect of a venture is as exhilarating as it is daunting. The fear of failing can form a significant barrier to innovation—that very threat that their vision cannot be realized—paralyzing innovation and affecting the diffusion of innovative concepts. Overcoming this barrier requires a paradigm shift. Entrepreneurs should understand that failure is part of the game and not destructive; it only provides new opportunities rather than painful barriers. A successful entrepreneur knows that failure is not the opposite of success but a stepping stone to success.

Stress to Conform

In such a hostile environment, there is often perceived overwhelming pressure by all to toe the established line of what is expected. This, in its thrust for short-term profitability and quick productivity, tends to discourage risks and creativity. Entrepreneurs may feel bound to play it safe and depend on tried-and-tested methods rather than move into uncharted waters.

Such pressure for conformity stifles creativity, limiting the journey of a new invention and plan. Entrepreneurs have to be bold enough to break free from the ordinary course, question conventional wisdom, and work hard toward their objectives with persistence to remove such barriers.

Resource Constraints

Entrepreneurs face the challenge of resource limitation during the implementation of creativity. With the difference from the big established business entities that have all the financial wherewithal and the stock of other various resources at their disposal, entrepreneurs more often than not run on a deficit of economic means and labor force. This can be a source of a scarcity mentality and finally dwell on creativity because, with the feeling in them, they feel constrained with such a low level of resources.

Yet, resource constraints may be the very stimulants for growth. Necessity is the mother of invention, and entrepreneurs are driven to find "out of the box" solutions to their predicaments.

Exhaustion and Overwhelm

A good entrepreneur views their constraints as an opportunity for ingenuity in problem-solving to make the constraints work for them. The constant pressures an entrepreneur faces have the potential to result in physiological and psychological breakdowns, such as fatigue or a feeling of being overburdened. Most entrepreneurs multitask: process management is done with marketing and sales. The constant stress and straining hardly allow for any time or energy to be at hand for creative work. Furthermore, this hustle and work culture often help develop a gait toward exhaustion: businesspeople feel it necessary that in life, one has to work oneself to the bone. Conquering this difficulty requires business owners to focus on self-care and wellness.

It has to do with acknowledging the value of rest and the pleasure of taking breaks and retreating to re-energize. Mind and business owners should make their well-being a top priority in order to unleash their creative thinking potential.

Business Culture

Failing to build a culture of innovation within a company can be a substantial obstacle for business owners. In several organizations, creative thinking takes a rear seat to effectiveness and efficiency. The power structure and inflexible procedures can smother advancement, as workers really feel limited by a lack of freedom and flexibility to explore innovations. Additionally, the fear of failure and an unwillingness to challenge the norm can produce a culture of uniformity where creative thinking is inhibited.

Unlocking Your Creativity as an Entrepreneur

Unlocking creativity as a business owner is a demanding process that includes incorporating cutting-edge reasoning for organizational success. In the busy and demanding landscape of entrepreneurship, creative thinking functions as a driver for development, analysis, and excellence. Right here, we will certainly discover different approaches and strategies for business owners to harness their creative thinking, grow a culture of development, and access opportunities.

Establish a Creative Mindset

Cultivate an imaginative way of thinking as a business owner by accepting inquisitiveness, visibility, and resilience. Master the ability to come up with an idea that is free to accept change and more open to expansion when faced with unforeseen challenges and difficulties. Be curious and new to novel situations, perspectives, and experiences. Draw inspiration from all possible sources: through arts, literature, scientific explorations, and nature. Embrace ambiguity and vagueness for discovery and innovation. Build resilience in the face of misfortune—creative thinking is often called up to find the most conducive environment in challenging situations. In this fresh way, a new form of innovative thinking will be born. It will grow your power in the entrepreneurial capacity and drive added value in your service from the prowess of innovation.

Accept Constraints as Opportunities

Restrictions are an all-natural component of the business trip; however, they can additionally act as stimulants for creativity and development. Welcome constraints as chances to think outside the box and discover ingenious services to obstacles. Use constraints such as time, budget plan, or resources to preserve creativity and promote critical reasoning. Encourage your staff members to welcome constraints as innovative obstacles instead of barriers, equipping them to discover extraordinary strategies and unlock brand-new opportunities.

Cultivating a Culture of Creativity

As a business owner, you have the power to define the culture of creative thinking as well as development. Encourage open interaction, cooperation, and idea-sharing amongst your staff members. Create room for conceptualizing and trial and error where people really feel encouraged to discover brand-new ideas and challenge the norm. Commemorate creative thinking and acknowledge the contribution of team members who show innovative reasoning as well as analytics.

Further, creative thinking is an effective tool for situation analysis in the business context. Motivate your staff members to approach difficulties with creativity and resourcefulness, equipping them to think outside the box as well as check out non-traditional options. Develop an encouraging atmosphere where people really feel comfortable taking risks as well as trying out novel situations. Offer resources and support to help with creative problem-solving, such as accessibility to training, tools, and innovation. By encouraging innovative problem-solving, you can eliminate barriers and take advantage of possibilities for innovation in your company.

CHAPTER 7:
Nurturing Your Well-Being

Entrepreneurship is an Inside Job. The journey of entrepreneurship is more than just these outward success stories and business accomplishments. More importantly, it's about taking care of yourself- the foundation on which your entire entrepreneurial venture is erected. Now is the time to explore what has been missing in this equation- an element of personal care, which will coach you on how to balance the demands of your business with the need to nurture your physical, emotional, and mental well-being.

In the world of entrepreneurship, where there is a whole lot of hustle and bustle and entrepreneurs are fighting to stay ahead, it is very easy to neglect your well-being. Some people get so engrossed in their businesses, lost in long hours or hard work and pressure, that even when their body is signaling that it needs to rest, they deny their body its right to rest. "It's just that I am a workaholic.", I hear people say that a lot, and I wonder if they realize that "body is not firewood". Now, don't get me wrong, I am not against working hard to achieve success, but you need to understand that whether you accept it or not, your physical, emotional, and mental well-being contributes greatly to your success. When you are physically, emotionally, and mentally sound, you stand a better chance of achieving a higher level of productivity than if you are not. In this chapter, you will learn how to nurture your emotional well-being while thriving for success.

By properly taking care of yourself, you will better be able to increase your quality of life, develop your ability to lead with greatness and have the creative stamina to fuel your business. Some practical tools and techniques are provided in this chapter for dealing with stress, warding off burnout, and incorporating self-care quickly into the daily routine. Understanding and taking the proper care of your well-being is not just beneficial; it is necessary to have the stamina and resilience needed to push through for long-term success in the grueling world of entrepreneurship.

Understanding Emotional Well-being

Emotional well-being in entrepreneurship delves even further than just the feel-good aspect of it, opening how an individual garners, appraises and controls emotions as they seek success in the business. This includes how one can handle stress, overcome disappointment, and have a meek attitude given the entrepreneurship barriers.

What Is Emotional Well-Being?

In more simplified terms, good emotional health involves being self-aware and able to accept your feelings and, at the same time, manage those same feelings. It goes on to include how ideas and behavior are touched by feelings and the application of such knowledge to think and act productively. It is also how you manage your emotions effectively so that balance is achieved within both your private and professional worlds.

Emotionally healthy entrepreneurs are pretty resilient to challenges. They are seen as an opportunity to keep making even more strides and building one. Life does not give them lemons but a spirit of being positive and tenacious—those ignited by the spirit of tenacity. They will go through adversities, learn from them, and grow into entrepreneurs.

Emotional Well-Being as a Fuel for Productivity and Success

Another need that should be in the entrepreneur's character is emotional well-being, as this is very important and affects immeasurably the productivity and success of the entrepreneur in the long run.

- **Better Decision Making**: Emotionally balanced entrepreneurs will be able to make clear and objective decisions. This allows them to make more planned and productive decisions, and they are less likely to be acted upon by impromptu moments or judgment clouded.

- **Increased Resiliency**: In the journey of entrepreneurship, there are various cases of uncertainties and failure. Through a good understanding that business is a survival game of the fittest, entrepreneurs who have emotional reasoning will do pretty well. Rather than relent in their effort in the face of challenges, they see challenges as an opportunity to step back and reflect on the whole situation so that they can make better decisions to help them grow. Their persistence and resilience during difficult times help them move forward and make progress.

- **Enhanced Creativity and Innovation**: Emotional well-being creates a healthy environment where creativity and innovation can flourish. When entrepreneurs are well emotionally, they may think more freely, explore new ideas, and develop their businesses.

- **Effective Communication and Collaboration**: Having healthy relationships is very important in the world of entrepreneurship. When an entrepreneur is emotionally balanced, it helps them develop and maintain relationships. Entrepreneurs who understand and navigate through their emotions and those of others can communicate effectively, handle issues constructively, and build solid partnerships.

- **Healthy Professional life**: Sometimes, for entrepreneurs, the line between their professional and personal lives is usually blurred but having emotional well-being can help them create a balance by reducing burnout and providing energy and focus for both professional and personal activities.

As an entrepreneur, you must prioritize your well-being. This is very important if you plan to be successful in a world full of competition. When you are emotionally well, you can make clear and informed decisions that will foster the growth of your business and also help you build healthy relationships.

Why Do People Struggle to Prioritize Their Well-Being?

Entrepreneurship is typically seen as a journey of endless hustle, where success is accomplished with round-the-clock dedication and sacrifice. Nonetheless, this "hustle culture" can take a toll on business owners' well-being. In spite of comprehending the relevance of self-care and health, several business owners battle to focus on their own health and happiness.

Pressure to Succeed

Among the major reasons that business owners battle to focus on their health is the tremendous pressure to do well. Beginning and running a service is incredibly tough, and business owners frequently feel like they need to work harder and longer than anybody else to attain their objectives. Therefore they might disregard their very own health for working longer hours and handling even more obligations.

The pressure to be successful can stem from various sources. It might originate from investors who anticipate a return on investment. It might stem from consumers who anticipate premium products or services. Plus, it might originate from society at large, which commonly relates success with lengthy hours and effort.

Lack of Work-Life Balance

Business owners typically have a hard time keeping a healthy and balanced work-life equilibrium. When you're running your very own company, it can be tough to switch off and detach from the job. There is always an additional e-mail to respond to or an additional issue to resolve. Consequently, business owners might find themselves working lengthy hours, compromising time with loved ones, and ignoring their very own health while doing so.

The idea of work-life balance can seem like a remote desire for numerous business owners. With many demands on their time and capacity, it can be tough to find time for leisure and self-care. Nevertheless, disregarding work-life balance can bring about burnout, reduced performance, and, eventually, failure.

Interest and Drive

Many business owners are driven by a deep enthusiasm for their jobs. They like what they do and agree to make sacrifices to see their vision become a reality. But such drive and energy could also be a bane. This is what may drive entrepreneurs to work hard and yet neglect their very own well-being just to get a task done.

Interest and drive are vital for success in entrepreneurship. They offer business owners the power and inspiration they require to overcome difficulties, take threats, and remain in the face of difficulty. Nonetheless, when taken to the extreme, enthusiasm and drive can result in burnout, poor health and wellness, and negatively affected partnerships.

Uncertainty and Stress

Running a company is naturally demanding, and business owners typically need to handle a high degree of unpredictability on a day-to-day basis. From rising and falling profits to unforeseen difficulties, there's constantly something to fret about when you're running your very own organization. This continuous anxiety, together with unpredictability, can take a toll on business owners' psychological and physical health, making it challenging to

The unpredictability and anxiety of entrepreneurship can be frustrating. It can keep business owners up at night, make them question themselves, and bring about feelings of stress and anxiety along with clinical depression. Without correct coping tools in place, this tension can spiral unmanageably, bringing about burnout and also, eventually, failure.

Societal Expectations

Business owners usually really feel stress from society to regularly keep hustling or grinding. There's an extensive idea that if you're not working 24/7, you're not really devoted to your organization or your objectives. Consequently, business owners might really feel guilty or self-conscious for taking some time off to concentrate on their health, being afraid that they will certainly be evaluated or viewed as careless.

The pressure to continually work can be ruthless to people, both themselves and others. They might feel like they need to work harder and longer than anyone else in order to be effective.

Lack of Time

Running a company is exceptionally taxing, and business owners typically feel like they do not have adequate time to focus on their well-being. In between handling everyday procedures, taking care of management jobs, and managing unexpected obstacles there's commonly extremely little time left over for self-care as well as leisure. Consequently, business owners might neglect their very own health to concentrate on their company.

How to Manage Stress and Anxiety

As an entrepreneur, you are responsible for a large amount of paperwork, projects, workshops, and other tasks. Keeping all of these things in check and not allowing the anxiety and tension to overwhelm you takes skills and a mindset that does not tend to affect your level of energy and creativity. Identifying what causes you stress can help you choose what you should do to relieve it. However, most of the time, it is a combination of factors, some of which you may be unaware of consciously. It appears that entrepreneurship and stress go hand in hand. Starting and growing a successful business can come with mental stress symptoms such as anxiety, sadness, restless nights, changes in weight, and other health issues. These symptoms are not strange, nor are they new. However, these consequences are unnecessary and are not a prerequisite for becoming a successful entrepreneur. However, you do need to be aware of any stress signs and know how to handle them. The first step is to identify the cause of the stress and anxiety. It could be the workload and responsibilities you have to deal with or the financial state of your business, especially for startups. This may be due to the pressure to survive in the rat race of entrepreneurship because most of the competitor companies have stood tall and firm due to the overtime put in. Maybe you want a proper support system, or you require a team. This stands out as the reason for the imbalance between your professional and personal lives. Whatever it is that causes you stress and nervousness; you have to identify that first before you move forward to eliminate it. Here's what you can do to manage stress and anxiety:

Above all, establish a strong network. Entrepreneurship is a lonely job, and one will need a sense of support from friends, family, advisors, and fellow business owners with whom to share critical psychological support. Surrounding oneself with people who understand the challenges one is going through can give insight, motivation, and points of view during rough times. Regularly contacting this group of people through meetings, phone calls, and even online forums can help alleviate the sense of isolation and bring reassurance during moments of doubt.

In another aspect, self-care is entirely central to caring for tension and anxiety. Deprivation of the body of self-care is usually because of their quests to become entrepreneurs, but instead, deprivation only intensifies the amount of stress being felt. Among the ways to counter tension and anxiety among entrepreneurs is through regular physical exercises, proper diet, and enough sleep; these work comprehensively for a much healthier physiological and emotional well-being. In addition, relaxation techniques, including meditation, deep breathing exercises, and mindful techniques, should be incorporated into routine life to reduce anxiety in a person's mind.

Time management is yet another critical factor because, truly, running a business often gets to the point where one just feels overwhelmed with the result of a constant sense of urgency, anxiety, and stress. Good time management related to making choices on what to work on, priorities, and setting achievable objectives and responsibilities that can be delegated will help business owners recover their time. Devices and methods that enable productivity to be kept within the proper levels—such as time blocking or the Pomodoro Technique—will help a person stay focused on performance so that anxiety does not rise.

A healthy work-life balance is an imperative factor in the successful avoidance of burnout and the proper development of stress-handling techniques for the business owner. As much as it may sound very tempting to take up all the available time and energy for building the business, it might result in forgetfulness of personal relations and leisure activities that might be damaging to the psychological and mental states. Boundaries should also be set between job and personal life, with scheduled time for downtime and activities away from the source of work to remain balanced and keep burnout at bay. Having interests and outside hobbies in addition to the entrepreneurial journey is an excellent source of priceless rest, developing creativity and perspective, which contribute to the general health status.

Besides the mentioned positive strategies, business owners should inculcate effective systems of dealing with anxiety or worry as and when it occurs. This could be through positive self-talk, reframing negative thoughts, or, if need be, through professional help. Appropriate professional help, including the treatment, therapy, and training in dealing with tension and stress, can therefore be realized to make it easy to deal with anxiety and, by extension, to bring to fruition healthy and balanced coping techniques in business owners to better handle the psychological difficulties of entrepreneurship.

The practice of mindfulness and being present in the practice itself dramatically removes the feeling of overwhelm, stress, and anxiety. The practice of entrepreneurship involves multitasking and requires one to anticipate future challenges, which may lead to overwhelm, stress, and fear. An illustration of this is in the instance of using some mindfulness strategies, in which one can focus on today, let go of the fears for tomorrow, and, in effect, stay grounded so that anxiety levels are consequently brought down. One uses these tools while riding the ups and downs of entrepreneurship. However, strategies like mindfulness enhance the capacity to focus, and one of the ways a person continuously increases decision-making capabilities is through improving focus.

However, stress and anxiety are by-products of nature in any entrepreneurial journey, just that they can be tackled well with proper methodologies in place.

Soothing Anxiety Within Your Team

As an entrepreneur, the necessity of stress, anxiety, and worry reduction within your work team cannot be overestimated, yet dramatically underappreciated. Here is how you can do that:

First and foremost, it encourages openness of communication. Encourage the staff to express their concerns, share their ideas, and tell of any problems they may be having. Create a culture of openness and support that enables staff members to really feel valued as well as seen, decreasing the feeling of being overwhelmed, stressed, and anxious. Routine group conferences, personalized check-ins, and anonymous feedback systems can help with open interaction and guarantee that every person really feels listened to and understood.

Secondly, where the expectations are not clarified, setting clear targets and expectations is likely to contribute to the anxiety and perceived sense of complexity. Outlying the objectives, deadlines, and performance measures will guide employees on what they are expected to do and how to be involved in learning. Moreover, regular feedback and the recognition of achievement will enhance a sense of purpose and motivation, further ensuring that tension is reduced and the team's spirits go up.

Thirdly, a culture should be created in the workplace that is supportive and healthy and will reduce significant levels of stress and anxiety among employees. Promote teamwork and compassion in the team, respecting differences and being inclusive. Belonging and unification reduce feelings of isolation by encouraging a supportive environment where employees can reach out for help and support each other.

Encouraging work-life balance can help reduce work and workplace anxiety. To enable the employees to take breaks during which they can rest, have personal time to take care of themselves, and set their work from their personal life boundaries. Flexible work schedules, including telecommuting or the provision of flexible time, allow workers to manage work with other commitments, hence reducing instances of anxiety and generally promoting one's health.

Lastly, showing resilience, positivity, and psychological awareness establishes the tone for the group and strategies that ease the tension. By modeling healthy and balanced coping systems as well as a positive state of mind, you can produce a helpful and boosting workplace that builds resilience and recognizes team effort, eventually minimizing tension, stress, and anxiety within the group.

CHAPTER 8:

Building a Healthy Workplace

As you learned in the previous chapter, self-care is an essential aspect of your overall well-being. You now know that to be fulfilled as a person and to be a successful professional, you must have your own physical, emotional, and mental health in check. You have built on this foundation of self-care so that you can now extend this care to others. First, you have to create a place that works for you; next comes making a healthy workplace for others so that your business can really grow. In this chapter, you will learn how to develop a positive work environment that positively impacts the well-being of your people and your productivity and creates a culture of mutual respect and support.

As a business owner with staff members, it's crucial to acknowledge that promoting psychological health and wellness in the office is not simply a moral necessity but likewise a deliberate decision. Psychological wellness includes an individual's emotional, mental, and social state of being. It is beyond the lack of mental disorders and consists of aspects such as joy, satisfaction, and resilience. At the workplace, mental health affects work interpersonal relationships, productivity, and general work satisfaction. The recognition and handling of psychological well-being are crucial in any scheme that hopes to realize a healthy, balanced, and effective working environment. The mental health of your employees is tied directly to the success of your business.

Building a healthy workplace means creating an atmosphere in which people feel supported, valued, and empowered to do their very best work. In this chapter, you will learn ways to develop such a culture of well-being in your organization to establish policies that support mental health, promote open communication, and provide resources and tools so staff can better manage stress and balance between work and life. By embracing these principles, you drive engagement, innovation, and loyalty in the company, along with improving the well-being of your team.

Understanding the Impact of Work-Related Stress on Mental Health

Work-related stress is the most common malady in modern, fast-paced, high-stress work environments. Its damaging effect on workers' psychological health and well-being cannot be overemphasized. As depicted above, this has a direct effect on a business owner's laborer's well-being and, consequently, his efficiency.

Primarily, chronic exposure to the stress of a work nature could result in various consequent mental complications, including anxiety and depression. An employee under too much stress is likely to feel overwhelmed and irritable, almost like one would think if the tensions emanating from the job were insurmountable. This will result in physical symptoms of headaches, fatigue, and sleeping problems, thereby complicating the issues of mental health.

Besides, work stress commonly leads to the experience of burnout: a psychological, emotional, and physical condition emanating from excessive and prolonged stress. It affects not only the performance of a worker but his whole life as well. In this regard, businesspeople can quickly feel low motivation, low interaction, and even low job satisfaction from staff experiencing burnout.

Work-related stress can also influence the relationship an employee has at the workplace. Very worrisome employees will tend to be retracted, irritable, and sometimes even socially withdrawn, so they cannot effectively work in unison with other workmates and authorities in their working areas. This can cause stress and disputes and even create a gap in interaction.

Additionally, the influence of work-related tension involves and can impact the company at once. High degrees of stress and anxiety amongst workers can result in boosted absenteeism and presenteeism (when workers are literally existing but not completely involved or effective), together with turnover prices. This not only interrupts operations and performance but likewise affects turnover for businesses in regard to employment, training, and shed efficiency.

Along with the instant repercussions, persistent work-related anxiety can have lasting effects on staff member well-being. Studies have revealed that long-term direct exposure to stress and anxiety hormonal agents such as cortisol can enhance the danger of establishing significant wellness problems such as cardiovascular disease, high blood pressure, and body immune system problems. Business owners should acknowledge the prospective wellness repercussions of uncontrolled work-related stress and anxiety as well as take proactive actions to alleviate its effect on their staff members.

Creating a Healthy Workplace: Practical Tips for Entrepreneurs

As a business owner, promoting a healthy and balanced work environment is necessary for the health and performance of your staff members. A healthy workplace helps sustain the psychological well-being of a worker, cultivates a favorable business society, and sustains worker growth and development. Some practical suggestions and resources that any employer can implement to pave the way for a healthier work environment include, but are not limited to, the following:

Encourage Regular Physical Activity

Encouraging physical activity by integrating regular examples into the daily routines of employees, either through fitness workouts or team workouts, should prove a great help in overall health, well-being, and health. You could encourage or inculcate physical activity as a habit into the daily routine of each employee by giving him incentives in the form of fitness workouts, team workouts, or by subsidizing gym memberships. Introduce initiatives: Dare to bring in initiatives such as standing workstations, walking meetings, or exercise breaks, inspiring more moving moments throughout the day. Through exercise, fitness will be encouraged in the employee, and his physical health will improve while reducing stress levels and increasing productivity.

Develop a Culture of Workload Management

Workload management should involve critical requirements for the prevention of exhaustion and the reduction of demands on the health of employees. Employees are encouraged to prioritize objectives that must be done, set attainable targets, and share responsibilities as the nature of the situation dictates. Further, staff should be supported and resourced to manage their workload through targeted interventions that can include time management training and job priority-setting devices, or where demand is high, additional staffing resources. This will enable the employees to maintain a healthy balance between work and other aspects of their personal lives and, through the establishment of a workload-controlled culture, reduce vulnerability to health and well-being issues associated with stress.

Provide Mental Health Resources

Provide all your employees access to psychological well-being resources and support services to the best of your ability. It should be implemented in a policy framework that includes full medical insurance with psychological health and wellness services, employee assistance programs with private counseling and support, and workshops on stress and resilience.

Provide a Positive Work Environment

This creates a holistic work environment where employees feel appreciated and valued. It brings to the table recognition and celebration, both large and small, to enhance spirits and inspire. Encourage diversity and inclusion among team members so that every person feels like they belong.

Offer Wellness Initiative

Health programs, provided in association with the present health programs, ensure the physical and psychological well-being of the employees with gym membership, fitness training, and team-building activities. Healthy snacks and meals at the office and enough breaks are encouraged to ensure self-care.

Develop Clear Policies and Procedures

Develop formal policies and procedures for health and wellness in the workplace for approved leaves, vacation times, and health and wellness-friendly office accommodations for employees with disabilities or chronic health and wellness concerns. Disseminate information to employees to keep them knowledgeable about what they are entitled to and expected to do.

Encourage Social Connections

Help generate opportunities for the workers, in which they can be connected into a social partnership with other associates. Arrange team-building tasks and social occasions along with networking opportunities to promote a feeling of openness as well as team effort. Encourage partnership and share assistance amongst your workers.

Monitor and Evaluate

Consistently keep an eye on and assess the efficiency of your workplace health initiatives. Receive feedback from your workers through surveys, focus on teams, or individual conversations to recognize areas for improvement and make needed changes. Continuously aim to develop a workplace environment that promotes wellness, contentment, as well as success.

Implement Flexibility and Autonomy

Providing adaptability and freedom in how workers handle their jobs can add to a much healthier and more effective office atmosphere. Whenever feasible, allow staff members to have control over their job schedule and due dates. Another way to implement flexibility is by providing alternatives for remote jobs, flexible hours, or shorter working weeks to fit specific choices and requirements.

CHAPTER 9:

Overcoming Imposter Syndrome

The chapter opens up to the primarily vast silent challenge of Imposter Syndrome: a condition of constant self-doubt and fear of exposure as a fake, notwithstanding your apparent achievements. You'll find yourself in a better position to identify the signs of Imposter Syndrome; you'll know how this can silently weaken your confidence and professional growth. Through practical strategies and insightfully helpful guidance, you'll learn how to face and then conquer such feelings to turn self-doubt into self-confidence. By the end of this chapter, you will be confident in embracing your success, positively building your self-image, and moving forward on your entrepreneurial journey with renewed confidence in yourself and your abilities.

It has been estimated that nearly 70% of people will experience signs and symptoms of impostor phenomenon at least once in their life. Impostor syndrome has been linked to a variety of age groups, including mature professionals in the workplace, graduate students, and high school pupils. Most research indicates that imposter syndrome appears to be more common in women and disproportionately affects underrepresented minorities and immigrants, while opinions on this matter are divided.

The idea of impostor syndrome is that you're not actually an impostor, but you just think you are an impostor. It is associated with active self-depreciation of one's efforts, goals, and achievements, and even going as far as one's existence. The concept behind impostor syndrome is undervaluing and minimizing one's potential, skills, talents, and values, especially in comparison to what the external environment sees. Impostor syndrome is a mismatch between internal beliefs about oneself and the external objective evidence of his/her personality, capability, and achievement.

A person with imposter syndrome is a harsh self-critic and could be seen as a self-abuser. This is because the impostor syndrome involves meeting endless torments and afflictions on oneself by oneself over flaws, weaknesses, or imperfections that may exist only in his/her mind. The bounding negative impact of this inner struggle on one's quality of life is enormous. Interestingly, it has been observed that the most skilled and competent people tend to underestimate their own talent, skill, and even worth.

According to Jennifer Hunt (2020), Impostor syndrome does not exist in isolation but sits at one end of the spectrum, with the opposite end being egotism. People falling under this category (egotism) are over-confident and have high opinions of their contributions—despite external objective evidence suggesting that they are either normal or even under-performers. In other words, they are extremely self-appreciative. It is called the Dunning-Kruger effect. The Dunning-Kruger effect is probably what convinces a person who cooks meals for just her family's consumption (on a small scale) to think she can open a line of restaurants without training. So basically, at one end, underachievers or barely achieving persons interpret their performance as high and rank themselves better than others, and at the other end, high achievers underestimate their own abilities and performance to the point of near incapacitation.

Impostor syndrome is investigated in response to specific stimuli and occurrences. It is an experience that a person has, not a mental disorder, and as such, it can be overcome. Research shows that feelings of insecurity can come as a result of an unknown environment and unexpected change. Lower self-confidence and faith in one's own ability may result from this.

How to Recognize the Impostor Syndrome

Pauline Rose Clance—who, with Suzanne Imes, coined the term "impostor syndrome"—also published a short assessment to determine the level of impostor tendencies. A person with impostor syndrome must exhibit at least two of the following six criteria, according to Clance's 1985 study, which defined the imposter phenomenon.

Types of Impostor Syndrome

It can emerge in a variety of ways, each with its own distinct features. Listed below are some frequent types of imposter syndrome:

- **The Perfectionist**: Perfectionists establish extremely high standards for themselves and frequently feel like failures if they do not fulfill them. They believe that every minor error indicates ineptitude; thus, they always strive for perfection. Despite their achievements, they credit them to other causes rather than their own ability, worrying that they will never be good enough.

- **The Expert**: Experts assess their competence based on what they know or can do. Although they are continuously seeking new knowledge and abilities, they never feel as if they have learned enough. Even when they are extremely competent and inferior in comparison to others. This group of individuals is afraid of being revealed as a newbie. Therefore, they avoid situations in which they may not have all the answers.

- **The Natural Genius**: Natural geniuses believe that if they are truly skilled, tasks should come naturally to them with little effort. They have high expectations for themselves and are ashamed when they struggle or have to work hard to achieve anything. They attribute their achievement to luck or external forces rather than appreciating their own efforts. This might create a cycle of procrastination and self-doubt.

- **The Soloist**: Soloists prefer to work independently and believe that seeking assistance or support is a sign of weakness. They believe they should be able to handle everything on their own and are afraid that seeking help will reveal their lack of competency. Even when they accomplish success, they struggle to accept it since they believe they didn't do it all by themselves.

- **The Superwoman/Superman**: Superwomen and men are high achievers, driven to be perfect in whatever they do, whether at work, in their relationships, or in personal projects. Most often, they feel they must play so many roles and play them well. They think that failing in one aspect means they are losers or that it becomes their excuse for not performing in another. Although accomplished, they cannot enjoy their accomplishments and sometimes believe that they are under much strain to perform more tasks.

So, the first step to conquering imposter syndrome is realizing what type you have. It sets a healthier perspective regarding success and failure, for one, to recognize that such feelings are normal and have nothing to do with how competent you are. Perhaps looking in the company of friends, family, or a therapist will change such negative thought spirals for the better—yet with more doubt. However, it doesn't need to be what defines your worth or limits your potential.

Understanding Impostor Syndrome in Entrepreneurship

This impostor syndrome can be a massive setback for young entrepreneurs in trying to figure out this market that constantly keeps changing. However, remember that 84% of entrepreneurs report experiencing the same, so take note that this problem is shared with other individuals. Impostor syndrome makes it hard for young entrepreneurs to develop themselves personally or professionally. It paralyzes the decision-making process, and lack of confidence, combined with self-doubt, hampers the road to progress. Fear of being construed as incompetent, or worse, a cheat, hampers the way to networking and building connections.

One of the most profound relations of entrepreneurship is with uncertainty and risk; many entrepreneurs start their ventures unaware of whether they are going to succeed. They walk into territories where no man has walked before and experience challenging situations of varied sorts. In such a scenario, it would be pretty natural for one to be kept in self-doubt and have impostor syndrome arise. Overcoming impostor syndrome in entrepreneurship can be quite a challenging yet integral journey to the flourishing of any entrepreneur. The impostor syndrome is most common in an entrepreneur, the person who has to work almost all of the time in an uncertain environment, with huge risks on the line and very high expectations. Below, we will detail how such a syndrome corresponds to the very concept of entrepreneurship and define a way out.

Types of impostor syndrome that an entrepreneur can go through:

- **Feeling of Inadequacy**: An entrepreneur invests so many resources of time and effort into a venture that he may begin to doubt his capacity as a good leader, a good decision maker, or one who can contain a setback, fearing that any misstep would be self-affirmative of these feelings of inadequacy.

- **Comparison with Peers**: The entrepreneurial space is abuzz with overnight success and high-flying individuals, which usually makes entrepreneurs compare their stories to those of their peers. If they do not really measure up to the success level of their peers, this may lead to discounting their own achievements as a fluke or caused by some aspect other than their own business acumen.

- **High Expectations**: As the expectations to perform are high, the pressure surmounts from the inside-out: from investors, customers, and stakeholders. Such pressure to meet expectations and deliver could lead these entrepreneurs to feel like impostors and start asking themselves if they are really up to it.

- **Isolation**: Entrepreneurship may be a lonely pursuit, especially for the solopreneur or the leader of an early-stage start-up. Doubts multiply if there is no one around with whom to share struggles and decisions, with that entrepreneur facing problems and choices entirely alone, with nobody to validate their thoughts and assure them.

Strategies for Overcoming Impostor Syndrome in Entrepreneurship

Though it is such a personal battle in fighting impostor syndrome, strategies are readily available and applicable that may help entrepreneurs relieve themselves of the burden of it:

1. **Acknowledge and Accept Feelings**: The first response to handling the Impostor Syndrome could be to acknowledge and admit that such a thing is happening to you. It's okay to feel doubtful and insecure at times. Do admit it recognize that this is normal, but never let it make you think unsuited to do business.

2. **Challenge Negative Self-Talk**: Catch yourself when your mind starts delivering the entire negative self-talk, and fight back with all the positivity you know. Remember your strengths, the achievements during your business life, and the value you bring to your business and industry. What's more important is putting such perceptions to rest.

3. **Set Realistic Goals**: You should define your goals for yourself and your business. Divide the large tasks into small and realistic goals. That makes you monitor while giving a sense of victory, as you can celebrate success by realizing targets or goals. This method leads toward a feeling of achievement and, in return, raises the level of confidence.

4. **Seek Support and Feedback**: Engage with a supportive community of mentors, peers, and other entrepreneurs who can offer you guidance, wisdom, and constructive critical feedback. Sharing the weight with others may perhaps even provide validation from them, triggering recovery from feelings of loneliness or impostor syndrome.

5. **Celebrate Successes**: No matter how little it is, celebrate success. Think back about the strength of that success and the

sweat that came through tears. Keeping a journal or a gratitude log might be a powerful tool to realize progress and reinforce confidence.

6. **Embrace Failure as Growth**: Understand that failure is an event, not a person; that failure is so much part of the process and not at all a statement regarding the quality of the individual's self-portrayal or ability. Don't get bogged down by failures; instead, unearth excellent lessons from such failures and use them for personal and professional growth. The power of a growth mindset is in learning, adapting, and persevering through the adversities one will face.

7. **Focus on Continuous Learning**: Never stop learning or developing yourself. Be curious; you will develop interest in new ventures, and you will have the inclination to learn the skills and knowledge that can be sold within your industry. When people have a growth mindset, they develop confidence and competence, and as such, they alleviate feelings of insufficiency.

8. **Practice Self-compassion**: Approach yourself with kindness and self-compassion. Try to be understanding and supportive toward yourself as a friend would be in the same circumstances. Incorporate self-care practices involving mindfulness, physical activities, and rest into daily routines to enhance mental and emotional well-being.

9. **Visualize Success**: Use the strength of your capability to visualize yourself achieving what you desire, conquering all your

adversities, and, in the end, running your successful business. Imagine yourself challenging all vibes, making significant moves, and eventually living your vision for your business. Thinking definitely will increase belief in self and motivation.

10. **Seek Professional Help if Needed**: Preferably that of a therapist or counselor, when the syndrome is much of a bother to your mental health and is otherwise affecting your performance at work. Therapy is very supportive and gives many insights and tools actually to work with impostors in a resilient way.

Impostor syndrome is a dark cloud in your entrepreneurial journey, pulling you toward success. Using these strategies will help you go past being an impostor and, therefore, unleash the full potential of being an entrepreneur because you have to be self-aware, resilient, and self-compassionate. After all, you are not alone in your struggle, and perceived flaws or insecurities do not gauge your worth. Then, feel free to embrace those unique talents, experiences, and perspectives as you forge confidently ahead in your quest to achieve entrepreneurial success.

Young entrepreneurs should learn the causes and triggers of imposter syndrome to successfully fight it. Positive mentality, celebration, seeking support, and building a support system are some of the few significant steps along the journey. It is assuredly not the absence of self-doubt that shows success as a young entrepreneur; instead, it is how one gets over doubt and still holds faith in oneself. One must accept each challenge, deal with each of them one step at a time, and trust the process that is embedded in reaching one's entrepreneurial goals.

Is Imposter Syndrome an Alien Phenomenon?

The business world, with its relentless forces and striving, is the greatest illustration of this phenomenon. An example is what Sheryl Sandberg, the operating officer of Facebook, does. In spite of her excellent job and countless successes, she has freely spoken about her battles.

Sandberg shares her experiences with self-doubt and the consistent fear of being exposed as a fraud. She often felt like she really did not belong, connecting her success a lot more to good luck than her very own capacities.

So also, Richard Branson, the owner of the Virgin Group, has actually admitted to experiencing impostor syndrome. In spite of constructing a multi-billion dollar empire, Branson has actually admitted to feeling like a fraud. He occasionally questions his very own capacities as well as frets that he will certainly be seen as a fake. Nevertheless, rather than allowing these sensations to consume him, Branson utilizes them as inspiration to work even harder and prove himself.

Sara Blakely, the owner of Spanx, is an additional instance of an effective business owner who has actually had a problem with impostor syndrome. Despite being among one of the most effective female-led companies worldwide, Blakely has talked about feeling like she is "faking it" as a business owner. Nonetheless, in spite of these sensations of self-doubt, Blakely has actually developed Spanx into a multi-million dollar company and has actually been called among Time magazine's 100 most significant individuals.

Also, Oprah Winfrey, the media magnate and TV personality, is another example of an effective business owner who has actually experienced impostor syndrome. In spite of her enormous wealth and popularity, Winfrey has actually admitted to feeling like a fraud. She often questions her very own capacities and frets that she does not deserve her success. Nonetheless, like several others who have actually experienced impostor disorder, Winfrey utilizes these sensations of question as inspiration to work harder and prove herself.

The tales of these successful business owners serve as an even among the most accomplished people. Nevertheless, they also reveal that it is feasible to conquer these feelings of self-doubt and attain wonderful things.

If you're battling with impostor syndrome, keep in mind that you're not the only one. Several successful business owners have actually experienced the very same feeling of self-doubt and inadequacy. The trick is to identify these feelings for what they are-- a typical component of the entrepreneurial journey-- as well as to not allow them to hold you back. Rather, utilize them as motivation to work harder, push yourself out of your comfort zone, and prove to yourself that you can attain incredible heights. As Sheryl Sandberg once said, "Feel the fear and do it anyway."

CHAPTER 10:
Building Strong Support Networks

The chapter is going to help you build a good support network that provides opportunities, nourishment, and strength. You are empowered to appreciate the fine art of intelligent networking, be in a position to learn how to acquire and also sustain such relationships that lead to mutual growth, and know how you can reach out for your network's help toward becoming a better professional and person. You will learn how this dynamic web of relationships can build into a support system that will help you ride out the tough times and capitalize on your successes as you journey through the entrepreneurial process.

In the business arena, relationships are not merely coincidental; they are the actual fabric for holding individuals, companies, and industries together. The value of relationships does not rest in mere transactions. It encompasses such factors as trust, commitment, and mutual benefit. Primarily, business is about people contacting other people and forging meaningful relationships that fuel cooperation, innovation, and progress.

The relationships in business have to work harmoniously with each other based on trust. Trust is the currency of effective business communications, underpinning every deal, negotiation, and partnership. When trust exists, connections thrive, cultivating open interaction, openness, and reliability. Trusted connections equip stakeholders to navigate uncertainties with confidence, recognizing that their counterparts will certainly act in their best interests. In addition, trust engenders loyalty, as companies and people focus on lasting connections over temporary gains.

Moreover, connections in the business world are linked with reputation. A positive track record is indispensable, acting as a magnet for opportunities and a guard against misfortune. Business relationships grow in an environment of mutual respect and integrity where stakeholders promote their dedication and make great on their promises. A good reputation preceded individuals and even organizations. It opens doors to brand-new collaborations, customers, and endeavors. On the other hand, a blemished reputation erodes trust and damages connections, resulting in missed opportunities and reputational harm.

Entrepreneurs acknowledge the significance of networking leverage their networks to gain access to resources, build tactical collaborations as well as gain beneficial insights from coaches and peers. Efficient networking makes it possible for business owners to increase their reach, build trust, know when to alter their strategy, and also open up doors to brand-new opportunities. This will now be explored in detail.

The Importance of Cultivating Support Relationships

In the demanding landscape of entrepreneurship, success is hardly ever a solo venture. Behind every prospering endeavor exists a network of support relationships that nurture, encourage, and move the business owner ahead. Growing these partnerships isn't merely an issue of benefit; it's a calculated essential that underpins the actual fabric of business success. Some of the reasons as to why these connections are important include:

- **Psychological Health and Well-being**: Business enterprise is an uncertain journey of challenges based on high-stress levels. The management burden, including highs and lows, may sometimes prove too heavy for the psychology of a business person. There are times when a good support network proves to be the real lifeline. Trusted close friends, mentors, or peers provide a confidential space for sharing questions, fears, and frustrations, reducing tension and providing protection against exhaustion. In addition, support networks contribute significantly to the general health and resilience of business people by encouraging an atmosphere characterized by compassion and understanding.

- **Access to Resources**: No entrepreneur can thrive in isolation; they require a diverse array of resources to fuel the expansion of their initiatives. Support systems make way for highly resourceful resources, such as funding, technical know-how, skills, and networks. For these reasons, mentors, as well as consultants, offer such well-to-access support out of many experiences while sharing wisdom and perspectives from many anglers offered through peers. In addition to that, deliberate networks created through beneficial partnerships provide a chance for new entrepreneurs to find new markets and distribution channels, as well as opportunities for cooperation. In this manner, nurturing relations can be said to be the only way resource constraints are surmounted, and speed-to-success can be made faster.

- **Feedback and Validation**: Entrepreneurs often operate in innovation and development. Such is the time when the input of others whom one trusts becomes a compass that leads one in the direction of success. Support systems help foster constructive criticism in pinpointing to business owners how they can tweak their ideas, methods, and products, considering insights gathered from their community. Whether that is testing a model, honing an analogy of the model for an organization, or validating the needs in a market, support from mentors, colleagues, and customers can help business leaders make more informed decisions to mitigate risk.

- **Collaboration and Partnership Opportunities**: In entrepreneurship, it is said that two heads are better than one. Encouraging connections leads the way for partnership along with collaboration opportunities that expand the reach and impact of a venture. By straightening with complementary businesses, organizations, or people, business owners can utilize synergies, pool resources, and deal with obstacles better. Joint ventures not only enhance the endeavor's capabilities but also foster innovation through the cross-pollination of ideas as well as technical know-how. From collaborations and strategic partnerships to co-creation initiatives, the opportunities for collaboration are limitless when business owners grow helpful connections.

- **Client Insights and Market Intelligence**: Successful business owners are skillful at comprehending and satisfying client requirements. Nonetheless, acquiring a deep understanding of consumer choices together with actions requires continuous engagement as well as discussion. Such support systems are critical in making a wide variety of perspectives and market insights available to a business owner. The feedback of the customers, market experts, and peers helps the business owners perfect their offerings, identify emerging trends, and be at the forefront of the competition. In addition, an active member of industry networks and communities allows business owners to develop deep and meaningful relationships with prospective customers and industry influencers, expanding their reach and influence in the marketplace.

- **Inspiration and Accountability**: Life is very challenging, and at times, it pushes one even beyond the limits of the most resilient individuals. It is at these moments that motivation and inspiring support from trusted comrades counts. The support networks become the source of inspiration, motivation, and accountability, reigniting the entrepreneur's desire to move on in pursuing their goals with renewed vigor toward overcoming hurdles. Be it celebrating success, navigating troubles, or staying the course in the face of uncertainty, the solidarity of the encouraging network equips business owners to remain focused, resilient, and relentless in their pursuit of success.

- **Strength and Adaptability**: Entrepreneurship is a vague and uncertain career in which entrepreneurs learn to walk through spaces they don't know. But that is where the strength of a support network can shine in times of crisis and disaster. Businesspeople create safety nets around them through deep, purpose-driven relationships predicated on trust and mutual benefit.

Be it financial support, psychological help, or advice on the best way to move forward, the solid supportive community emboldens entrepreneurs to ride out those storms and recover from failure, finally being able to come up more robust and more resilient than ever.

Mentors vs. Peers— Which Ranks in Priority?

Entrepreneurs work in a dynamic and uncertain business world where success typically requires the ability to navigate hurdles, seize opportunities, and make good decisions. Along the way, the support of coaches, advisors, and fellow business owners becomes equally important in bringing uniquely different perspectives and insights to the business owner and helping him to grow and succeed. While each type of relationship has its distinct value, none is inherently better than the others. Instead, it is the harmony and balance between mentors, experts, and peers that enable business owners to be armed with the ability to flourish in the business landscape.

With their treasure troves of experience and knowledge, coaches are very supportive and helpful to entrepreneurs. These trusted advisors can bring more perspective and years of accumulated practical experience to perceive the wave of the market and surmount the challenges with a game plan. Advisors will be sounding boards for the entrepreneurs, providing constructive criticism and encouragement as well as guidance, which helps in the development and growth of the entrepreneur.

Consultants provide specialized knowledge and domain know-how, offering focused support in specified areas of business expertise. This can be in the form of legal, financial, marketing, or technological advice, and it results in an informed decision-making process to minimize risks and maximize opportunities. Consultants support the advisor role with deep technological capability in tandem with strategic guidance, resulting in the fulfillment of immediate needs and challenges of the business.

While one can work with mentors and experts, peer networks provide a community, camaraderie, and a sense of responsibility that will ultimately result in success in business. Only peers can understand the unique challenges and obsessions faced by others starting small enterprises, offering empathy, inspiration, and practical advice based on shared experience. Peer networks promote partnership, advancement, and knowledge, providing business owners with a system to trade ideas, look for responses, and develop significant partnerships with similar people.

In addition, peer networks function as a source of objectives, track development together and remain focused on their goals. With casual checks, peer-led mastermind teams, or organized responsibility collaborations, business owners hold each other to high standards of efficiency, offering assistance and motivation to conquer barriers and stand firm through the ups and downs of entrepreneurship.

Essentially, while advisors, experts, and peers each bring one-of-a-kind points of view together with advantages to the entrepreneurial journey, none is naturally superior to the others. Instead, it is the harmony coupled with equilibrium between advisors, professionals, and peers that equips business owners with what it takes to flourish and prosper. By growing partnerships with advisors, professionals, and peers'; business owners have access to a varied community of support and accountability that increases their individual and professional development, drives their endeavors ahead, and boosts their opportunities for lasting success in the affordable landscape of entrepreneurship.

Glimpse into the Facebook Icon—The Dorm Room Startup

In 2004, a Harvard University sophomore named Mark Zuckerberg embarked on a journey that would change the world forever. Armed with nothing but a computer, some coding skills, and a desire to connect people, Zuckerberg launched what would eventually become the world's largest social media platform: Facebook.

Facebook's humble beginnings trace back to Zuckerberg's dorm room at Harvard. Alongside his roommates and fellow students, Andrew McCollum, Eduardo Saverin, Chris Hughes, and Dustin Moskovitz, Zuckerberg began working on a platform that would allow Harvard students to connect and interact online. What started first as a small idea rapidly spread to universes across North America and then across the world. In general, Facebook is all about communities. It is about relating to people, sharing experiences, and building relations. It is this level of community that facilitated a high level of success in the early days of Facebook and continues to be a driving force.

As an autotelic entrepreneur, Zuckerberg realized the value of community very early on. He realized that people needed to connect and tried to build a platform to allow people to do so materially. The establishment of a space for them to share thoughts, experiences, and interests enabled Zuckerberg to tap into this basic human need, hence creating a community different from all others.

Among the essential reasons for Facebook's success is the ability of this company to engage its customers. Since it started, was user-friendly, intuitive, and engaging. They realized that to build an influential community, they should create an exciting and involving place for people.

It is on Facebook where Zuckerberg created the People's Connect platform that revolutionized and changed the very way human beings communicate. Whether it is getting back to one's group of friends, keeping in touch with the family, or venturing out to meet new people with shared interests, Facebook has made it easy to connect with others and make meaningful relationships.

Zuckerberg didn't build Facebook alone; it was technology through which he materialized his idea. From the coding of the initial platform to building out the infrastructure to support millions of users, technology has played a crucial role in Facebook's success.

If there is any genuinely entrepreneurial story of Zuckerberg, it's one about community: whether you're an independent creator building a social alternative to the Great Machine of Surveillance and Control or getting ready to open a small business, remember to build community in your customers. You can nurture that sense of belonging and connection in your customers, which will hand you a loyal following through thick and thin. But building a community is not enough; you have to engage in the community. It means listening to your customers, responding to their feedback, and continually doing better by them. A relationship built with the community will see to it that there are pools of loyalty that will help your business flourish in the long run.

Obstacles to Building Strong Support Networks

Entrepreneur needs to build support networks which will guide and advise them as they journey to success. They, however, face numerous obstacles that hinder their capability to engage in a purposeful relationship with their advisor, coach, and peer, although they know the essence of the support. Many aspects hinder an entrepreneur from building a long-term support network, such as time limitations and the fear of refusal.

1. **Time Constraints**: Among the most common issues business owners face in creating support networks are time limitations. Starting and growing a business puts enormous demands on a business owner's time and energy, leaving small business owners little time and energy to expend on activities such as building their support networks or engaging in relationship-building activities that could benefit them. This could make it hard for entrepreneurs and business owners alike to focus on networking at a certain point. Therefore, they would easily miss the opportunity to connect with new potential mentors, advisors, and colleagues.

2. **Anxiety of Rejection**: Fear of rejection may also prevent entrepreneurs from associating with peers. The fear of being seen as not good enough or inexperienced may keep the entrepreneur from seeking the advice or help of more seasoned individuals. Additionally, the fear of being rejected may lead to entrepreneurs

procrastinating in initiating conversations or reaching out for help, thereby curtailing the expansion of their support networks.

3. **Geographic Constraints**: Geographical constraints can also limit the establishment of good support networks, particularly for entrepreneurs who are isolated or marginalized. This may mean that, due to access problems, one will not have the opportunity to be involved in any networking event, market seminar, or mentorship programs in a manner that will prevent the business owner from meeting potential coaches, advisors, or peers; equally, entrepreneurs operating businesses in rural areas may find it hard to get someone with like-minded interests and resources that can help that particular entrepreneur to keep their business afloat.

4. **Absence of Confidence**: The mere fact of entrepreneurship is a challenge, and self-doubt is only one of the common problems with which many entrepreneurs struggle. A business owner who lacks self-confidence will interact poorly while networking, often wondering if they are worth seeking help or guidance from another person. This lack of confidence manifests itself as an unwillingness to ask for help and a fear of appearing vulnerable or hesitant about engaging in networking activities.

5. **Mismatched Expectations**: Building strong support networks requires mutual respect between business owners and mentors, advisors, or peers. It also helps if what is expected from such interaction is well articulated at its inception. This is because

mismatched expectations can end up being significant hurdles for the development of critical relationships; the tendency of unrealistic expectations from the entrepreneur about what the mentor or the advisor can deliver causes a lot of frustration or stress if not met. Also, advisors or consultants could have expectations that don't meet the goals or top priorities of a business owner, hence not being involved or committed to the needs of such engagement.

6. **Restricted Access to Developed Networks**: Another critical challenge entrepreneurs face is limited access to developed networks or communities. Entrepreneurs new in a given industry or area may not find it easy to penetrate established networks or reach out to influential players. If entrepreneurs are not part of the relevant networks, they are likely to face challenges in accessing mentors, advisors, or even peers who can help provide the support or guidance needed.

7. **Networking Fatigue**: Sometimes, networking can be tiring— especially for introverted or socially anxious people. Continually attending networking events, reaching out to potential mentors or business advisors, and keeping up with one's peers can level most company owners' energy and motivation at some point. Networking fatigue might result in burnout and alienation as owners withdraw from such efforts of relationship building, missing significant opportunities for support and growth.

Approaches to Building Strong Partnerships

Whether it's nurturing connections with mentors, experts, or peers or creating collaborations with consumers and stakeholders, business owners can profit significantly from developing solid partnerships. Right here are a number of methods to construct as well as support partnerships:

1. **Specify Relationship Goals**: Before commencing their objectives and goals. Whether it's looking for mentoring, increasing their professional network, or cultivating collaborations, having clear objectives will certainly direct business owners in determining the sorts of connections they require to focus on along with support.

2. **Be Authentic and Genuine**: Authenticity is vital to developing purposeful partnerships. Business owners should aim to be genuine and clear in their communications, sharing their real intents, worth's, and desires. Genuineness promotes trust and credibility, laying the structure for long- lasting and equally meaningful partnerships.

3. **Give Value**: Building solid partnerships requires a give-and-take strategy. Business owners must make every effort to provide value and assistance to their counterparts, whether it's sharing know-how, offering support, or providing sources. By contributing favorably to the partnership, business owners can show their dedication and desire to contribute to the success of persons within their network.

4. **Stay Connected**: Consistent interaction is important for gradually supporting connections. Business owners must interact on a regular basis with their calls, whether via e-mail, telephone call, or in-person conference. By remaining attached and involved, business owners can maintain energy, enhance relationships, and maintain their partnerships active and growing.

5. **Be Proactive**: Building connections requires taking the initiative and embracing determination. Business owners ought to be proactive in connecting to possible mentors, consultants, or peers, starting discussions, and looking for opportunities to connect. Furthermore, business owners need to be consistent in their follow-up initiatives despite initial denials or troubles.

6. **Look for Diverse Perspectives**: Diversity enhances partnerships together with expands viewpoints. Business owners need to choose connections from varied backgrounds, markets, and experiences as they can provide fresh understandings, alternate perspectives as well as ingenious services. Welcoming variety nurtures creativity and fosters partnership and common learning in groups.

7. **Participate in Networking Events and Communities**: Networking events, market meetings, and online forums give business owners beneficial possibilities to connect with like-minded people and increase their professional network. Business owners need to proactively join relevant events and forums,

participate in discussions, and seek prospective partners and mentors.

8. **Provide Recognition and Appreciation**: Recognizing as well as valuing the sacrifices of others is necessary for show gratitude to their advisors, advisors, peers, and clients for their assistance, advice, and partnership. By recognizing their sacrifice, business owners reinforce bonds as well as nurture a culture of reciprocity and mutual respect.

9. **Be Patient and Flexible**: Building partnerships requires time and persistence. Business owners must hold their horses as well as understand and identify that significant connections cannot be hurried. In addition, business owners need to be versatile in their strategy for relationship-building, readjusting their techniques as well as assumptions as required to suit the characteristics of various connections.

CHAPTER 11:
Embracing Failure As a Steppingstone

As in the previous section, you explored establishing solid networks and knowing how these meaningful relationships, strategic alliances, or both could be a powerful tool to build upon your journey. When you have a sound network of contacts, you are better prepared to handle the humps and bumps associated with entrepreneurship. But even with the perfect plan and sometimes the ideal connections, failure is an inherent part of the entrepreneurial experience. As such, the chapter reframes failure as a way forward, not an end. How to take every setback as a learning curve and use it as the impetus for growth into that robust and resilient individual ready to take on today's business world is what you will learn in this chapter.

It is common knowledge that starting a business is hard, and ensuring continuity is even a lot more demanding, considering that businesses operate in an ever-changing market. Based on a 2023 survey of 10-year-old businesses in the United States, it was found that only 34.7 percent of businesses found between March 2013 and March 2023 were still in operation. Moreover, a review of the data on the U.S. Bureau of Labor Statistics (BLS) reveals that of 767,573 businesses commenced as of March 2020, only 489,540 were in existence as of March 2023. This implies that about 278,033 businesses were no longer in operation as of March 2023.

What this data does not tell you is how many of the entrepreneurs within the 278,033 commenced new business ventures in 2023 or the preceding years. This is relevant because entrepreneurs often implement an exit strategy but with the intention of starting a new enterprise. This means that the end of one business is the beginning of another in the world of entrepreneurship.

Sometimes, entrepreneurs plan businesses with the end in mind. On other occasions, life just comes together in a way that requires you to pursue a new business venture. Whether it is the former or latter, it is important to separate business success/loss from your personal identity. When you do so, you will be able to recognize that a loss or failure of a business does not define you as a person.

Do All Businesses Fail?

Of course not! There are businesses that have outlived their founders. Notwithstanding this, all businesses have down times—whether it is because of a recession, pandemic, or loss of revenue, employees, and market share, among others. It would not be far-reaching to say that the tax laws in some jurisdictions recognize the propensity for loss such that they allow businesses to deduct their losses when computing their tax liabilities.

However, some entrepreneurs are not easily deterred by failure or mistakes. This category of persons is able to recuperate from failure, pick up from blunders as well as adjust to transforming situations. They view all experiences as lessons to learn from and grow in both their personal lives and business.

Psychological Barriers to Failure

Understanding the psychological tools that can bring about failure for business owners is vital for identifying and also reducing prospective challenges in the business journey. While entrepreneurship is typically idealized as a path, it can take a toll on the mind. By investigating mental tools like these, business owners can much more effectively prepare themselves to deal with challenges and increase opportunities for success.

Probably one of the most dangerous mental tools that can drive a person to failure is perfectionism. The entrepreneur may set unrealistically high standards for himself and his projects: stressful and flawless management execution in all business details. While attention to detail in itself is a must, perfectionism can easily lead a person to procrastination, indecisiveness, and a fear of taking risks. One of the areas where the fear of failure tends to trap business owners is perfectionism. They freeze, unable to do anything, and allow those opportunities to slip by. To overcome such a mental barrier, it is essential to accept imperfections and embrace a continuous improvement mentality while learning from mistakes rather than striving for perfection.

Another mental tool that might fail is the fear of failing. An entrepreneur who has a fear of failing would most likely not take risks and would stay away from other potential problems and hassles. The ghost of impending failure often must be overcome by entrepreneurs. The possibility of founding a business may be exhilarating but can also, on the other hand, be intimidating. Fear of failure can act in many ways as a huge obstacle to creativity. It is the fear of one's idea not being realized or his efforts failing. Of course, no one would doubt that, in this respect, the fear of failure might turn out to be very self-limiting. It prevents the businessperson from finding new ideas, following an ambitious goal, and realizing one's full potential. The way to get rid of this barrier is simply to change the perception of failure as an all-natural element in the business journey, to embrace the lessons learned through setbacks, and to really see failure as a source of growth, learning how to become stronger. Effective business owners realize that the act of falling does not mean it is over; rather, it shows just another stepping stone on life's path to success.

Laziness is just another psychological tool that might defeat the success of a business. The owners procrastinate over critical tasks and decisions by succumbing to many distractions and procrastinating, rationalizing rather than focusing on set goals. Laziness can be brought about by many psychological factors that eventually reach the roots of perfectionism, fear of not succeeding, and lack of drive. Getting over this obstacle involves breaking down jobs right into more minor, workable actions, specifying target dates and responsibility actions, and developing self-control, where much could be done to conquer the impulse to procrastinate until the last minute.

Other standard emotional tools that can fail business people but not others are self-doubt and imposter syndrome. Business owners at the entrepreneurial level always doubt themselves; they begin by questioning their abilities and feel worthless in achieving success despite the evidence. Imposter syndrome eats into the self-esteem of the business owner, making them feel unworthy of the success achieved. Conquering this obstacle involves overcoming negative self-talk by reframing one's thoughts from limiting beliefs to building self-confidence through skills and experience.

Ultimately, fatigue is another psychological tool when foiling business success. In the course of this kind of engagement, an entrepreneur can get engrossed in work and forget his physical and mental health, thus moving toward fatigue, stress, and disappointment. Fatigue does not allow proper decision-making skills, creativity, and productivity—the three things a business cannot afford to do without if it is to succeed and not fail. This means taking care of oneself, setting limits together, and delegating so one is not prompted to throw oneself on the floor.

Reframing Failure as a Learning Opportunity

Failure is an inevitable part of the business journey. On the other hand, it does not have to be the end of the road. Instead of looking at failures as problems or objects of sympathy, businessmen can reconstitute them as lessons learned that would help in continuing development and progress combined with strengths. Through learning from mistakes and adapting their approaches, business owners can shift their state of mind to be able to tolerate, and hopefully even benefit from, the lessons brought about by failure.

Maybe the very first step that needs to be taken to learn from failure is to reframe the exact way of looking at it. Rather than viewing it as a judgment about one's abilities or potential, business owners can view failure as temporary, not an indication of failure or incompetence, but rather a pointer that an individual is pushing limits, taking risks, and challenging status. By regarding failure as a component of the business journey, business owners can minimize the preconceptions connected with obstacles and contribute to a society that promotes risk-taking.

The other important thing in reframing failure is gathering actual, helpful knowledge from the experience. Rather than looking at what went wrong or finger-pointing, business owners can look over the factors that contributed to their failure and learn how to learn from that. This requires asking such questions as what went right, what can be done differently, and what will be better. Being near to failing with an investigative and open frame of mind might provide business owners with insights that will help guide their decision-making and set their future strategies.

Secondly, thinking of failure as a learning process requires resilience and persistence. Entrepreneurship comes with its test nature. Failure is inevitable along the road. However, the reaction of a business owner to failure is what eventually determines their prosperity. Resilient business owners can recover from setbacks, eliminate roadblocks, and focus on their long-term goals. Through resilience developed (discussed in preceding chapters), an entrepreneur may go through the ups and downs with self-assurance and definiteness of purpose, knowing that failure is not the destination but just a detour on the way to success.

Moreover, redefining failure as a learning experience engages the willingness to ask for help and advice from others. An entrepreneurial life by nature could become lonely, but it should not be. Engaging advisors, experts, and peers with the ability to give input, perspective, and encouragement offers essential insights and support for overcoming entrepreneurship challenges. It also helps a businessperson get a fresh perspective on their failure by seeking feedback from others and pointing out blind spots that they may not know about.

Leveraging AI to Overcome Failure

Powerful tools have been incorporated in this digital age by artificial intelligence and modern technology to analyze failures and assist entrepreneurs today in grasping insights and making more informed decisions to recover. Its capacity is very significant and is applied to identifying patterns for future outcomes, improving decision-making, enhancement, and automation of routine tasks, among others usually facing business challenges.

The most significant advantage of AI is that it allows the entrepreneur to test vast amounts of information in a timely and effective manner. Entrepreneurs may use AI-based analysis to obtain vital insights from sources such as customer feedback, market trends, and financial metrics that shall quickly help in recognizing patterns and linkages that possibly caused their failure. For example, if a startup cannot take market share, AI analytics may go through customer responses, social media interactions, and sales data to infer reasons for the failure. That would help any entrepreneur to gauge customer preference, market dynamics, and pressure posed by competitors to calibrate strategies and changing offerings.

AI-based predictive analytics can also help entrepreneurs make a forecast and prevent failures that may occur in the future. AI tools analyze historical information to identify patterns for predicting future results and suggest actions leading to risk reduction. For example, AI can derive future demand from analysis of past sales data and customer behavior. Entrepreneurs can decide on pricing, marketing strategies, and product development accordingly with minimum risk.

In essence, decision-making is a critical part of entrepreneurship, and the incorporation of AI would go a long way in making it much better. AI tools seek actionable insights and recommendations drawn from analyzing data collected from varied sources. If a startup has trouble getting customers, analytics based on AI can help to analyze customer data and bring target demographics or suggest personalized marketing strategies. A data-driven approach helps avoid some of the most common pitfalls entrepreneurs make and make a few smarter choices to reduce failure.

Most entrepreneurs, at times, are bogged down by routine but time-consuming activities that are resource-intensive. Automation tools powered by artificial intelligence free up time that would otherwise be used, focusing on more strategic business areas. For example, AI chatbots can be used to respond to customer queries, provide support, and even process orders without human intervention. AI-powered data entry tools also make automatic data input and data analysis, something that would typically drain entrepreneurs of time and resources.

Coaching and feedback AI-powered tools provide personal insights and recommendations made to the entrepreneur on how to better their performance. These can be used to analyze past performance and identify what areas need improvement, providing tailor-made feedback and suggestions for growth. For example, AI mentorship systems can evaluate an entrepreneur's previous actions and recommend ways to improve their approach. What is more, AI analyzes interactions with customers to draw trends and advise on ways of offering improved products or services.

Customer experience underlies successful business for any company, and AI can play a significant role in its improvement. By using customer data and behavior analytics, AI-equipped tools assist entrepreneurs in better understanding customer needs, preferences, and sources of pain to make these experiences more individual and engaging. And so, customer service AI systems can provide information, detect the most typical problems, and react automatically, forwarding to real people if required. For instance, AI-powered recommendation engines suggest products or services based on the exact needs of each customer.

Additionally, AI plays a role in raising a culture of continuous learning within firms. Through data analysis on past failures and successes, the AI tools will quite easily point out developmental areas and suggest strategies for growth. Through AI-driven learning platforms, it is also easy to compare employees' performances and identify those who are not doing well, then recommend which optimal learning path they could take to build new competencies and thus improve the performance of promising employees. It can also use project data to analyze the bottlenecks and inefficiencies in a project and suggest changes in the process for productivity improvement.

Another big advantage of AI is real-time market analysis. This is where it helps provide real-time analytics to give entrepreneurs insights into market trends, customer preferences, and competitive landscapes, allowing them to make informed decisions and quickly alter their strategies. AI-based tools for market analysis can follow social media mentions, news, and online sources in general associated with a company's brand, its competitors, and industry trends in real-time. Entrepreneurs can draw deep insights, discover emerging trends, be updated on customer sentiments, and be one-up on the competition by analyzing data in real time.

The AI further assists in risk assessment and aversion through data analysis, therefore identifying possible threats to the business. It may evaluate financial data, market trends, and other indicative factors to point out risks, such as changing customer demand, supply chain disruption, or regulatory alteration. Early identification of these risks allows entrepreneurs to take some preventive measures, which will, in effect, reduce the risk and cushion such businesses from huge impacts.

Finally, AI enables innovation in terms of automating repetitive workflows, gaining an understanding of customer needs and preferences, and finding new growth opportunities. AI-powered innovation platforms can analyze vast amounts of market data, customer feedback, and countless other disparate information sources for latent customer needs, emerging market trends, and many other opportunities. Out of this, entrepreneurs can develop new products, services, and business models that differentiate the company from the competition and ultimately create growth.

CHAPTER 12:

Leveraging Social Media for Business Growth

Congratulations on traveling this amazing entrepreneurial journey through this book. Until now, you have explored the essentials of developing an entrepreneurial mindset, from cultivating resilience and setting effective goals to nurturing your well-being and building strong support networks. You've delved into how to foster creativity, embrace failure as a learning tool, and establish a healthy workplace culture. Each chapter has equipped you with critical insights and strategies to navigate the complex world of entrepreneurship successfully. Now, in Chapter 12, we turn our focus to a powerful driver of business growth in the digital age: *leveraging social media.*

Nowadays, social media has become part and parcel of businesses that aspire to achieve growth and success. An online presence can make or break a business. It can help one sail through to success, using effective social media marketing strategies to engage the audience and bring all potential customers into a lively community—moreover, measurement and analytics of social media success help refine those efforts and drive growth. The chapter will go into these aspects in enough detail, giving examples and hence providing insights toward realizing the full potential of social media.

The Power of Social Media in the 21st Century

In the 21st century, businesses are revolutionized in how they conduct themselves. Their change, in essence, from just a communicative channel to a paramount tool for business growth is what revolutionizes them. Having billions of active users on such platforms as Facebook, Instagram, and LinkedIn means that businesses can get a vast audience. The power of social media is that it makes communication easy and comprehensive. The platforms provide channels through which companies can communicate directly with customers and, in that line, create opportunities for engagement and feedback.

Today, social media has become a mainstream marketing platform. The most significant advantage of this media is that whatever size of business it is, it can reach even across the globe and market its products and services. The platforms enable instant interaction between business owners and customers, which helps in building a solid relationship to ensure brand loyalty.

What is more, social media provides a platform for businesses to understand the behavior and preferences of consumers. This data would help companies to have tailor-made marketing strategies towards the needs of their audience. Such targeted customization was not conceivable a few decades ago.

Consider how a beauty brand named Glossier made it with the leverage of social media in feeding growth. Technically, Glossier started as a blog, but just as quickly, it turned into a growing business with the use of social media. They were speaking with their audience on Instagram to build community engagement. They asked followers to share their beauty routines and product feedback to create community and trust. In a snap, thus, the ease with which they shared content assisted Glossier in adhering to their products and escalated brand visibility. Their social media presence also helped control their targeted advertisement, reaching the right audience.

Another strong case is Nike. Nike uses Twitter, Instagram, YouTube, and other social media websites to interact with millions of followers. Here, they post stories of athletes, new product launches, and inspiration to their followers. How campaigns such as "Just Do It" were related to challenges has greatly resonated and resulted in colossal engagement and loyalty. Nike also uses social media to solve customer inquiries and complaints, thus adequately solidifying its relationship with its consumers.

These are probably representative examples of how well companies can use social media to create intense connections with their target. All of them demonstrate the fantastic power of social media in the 21st century.

Building a Strong Online Presence

For good success in today's digital world, a solid online presence is paramount. This means being present on social media, having active profiles, a leveled-up website, and consistent branding across all online channels with a clear voice. It means being found where your audience hangs out and offering valuable content on things that are important to them.

Warby Parker is a great example. They found a way to make the social web work and established a highly viable social media presence through their approach to channels. Their Instagram account is one long page with high-quality shots of the product, user-generated content, and relatable stories that portray what the brand is about. It's also a means of customer service, as they majorly respond to questions and feedback on Twitter, which in turn helps them gain a fine reputation and build trust with the audience.

Another great example is Airbnb, which hopped onto social media to nail the science of storytelling through Instagram and Facebook. They post very scenic, impressive videos and photos of great and unique stays and experiences in travel that are inspirational and drivable to their audiences. They maintain a blog where travel tips and guidance establish further authority in the travel industry. An effective online presence—full of zest and appeal—has helped Airbnb increase its user base and build an active community of travelers.

These are instances that flesh out the need for a holistic online strategy. Most of the time, it is not about a solid online presence increasing business visibility but also about this being one of those elements that produces trust and loyalty toward customers. It's all about authenticity, engagement, and consistency across all online platforms so that your business stands out from the noise and litter of the digital landscape.

Strategies for Effective Social Media Marketing

An effective social media marketing strategy ensures maximum realization of your business goals. This implies that you need to know your audience and produce content based on the features of each platform. Now, let's see a few of the critical strategies in successful social media marketing using real-life examples.

Know-Your-Audience

The most critical premise of successful social marketing is knowing your audience. First of all, learn what and whom your audience is concerning demographics, preferences, and behaviors so that you can tailor your content to their needs and interests.

Example: Netflix employs high-level audience analysis in matters relating to their platform users, more so in making content recommendations and interacting via social media. In essence, they can interact with users about their favorite shows and movies, creating a sense of community and personalization through their Twitter account.

Consistent Branding

It portrays your identity and the content created by you. This is possible when the same logo, color themes, and brand voice are used consistently in all platforms.

Example: Coca-Cola, which retains the same brand image on all social media platforms. Their posts can be easily identified because they are done in their corporate red color, the logo is present, and their tone of voice is lively and friendly.

Engaging Content

It's very important to produce content that makes sense to the target audience. It may vary from educational, informational, to promotional posts. Visual content, such as images and videos, works best for that matter.

Example: GoPro is one of the best companies that deal with developing attractive visual materials. They share many user-generated videos and photos of adventurous and extreme sports that are done using their cameras, making them beautiful and just suitable for their brand image and audience.

Utilize Platform Features

Of course, every social media platform has its features, which can be used to an advantage depending on the level of engagement needed. These include the Stories on Instagram, Facebook Live, Twitter polls, and LinkedIn Articles.

Example: Starbucks is entirely engaging through its use of Instagram Stories and Highlights, sharing behind-the-scenes content, seasonal promotions, and customer stories, all of which make viewers want to keep looking at their stories for more.

Interactive and Real-Time Engagement

Engaging with your audience live can significantly enhance its interactivity and loyalty. Commenting, live sessions, polls, and Q&A all contribute to this.

Example: Wendy's is by far one of the most well-regarded Twitter accounts out there because of its sassy and on-time style of engagement. Most of the time, they respond to mentions and engage with followers, taking on trending topics, hence the development of a powerful and loyal community for this brand.

Influencer Collaborations

Work with an influencer whose brand aligns with yours to penetrate a more significant market and create a stand of credibility. They can present your brand most naturally and authentically to their followers.

Example: Daniel Wellington, with the example of a watch brand, has substantially benefited from the growth of the brand as a result of its influencer marketing. It has associated with fashion influencers on Instagram to create outreach to millions of followers and make the brand popular with a stylish aspirational image.

Data-Driven Decisions

For enhanced performance of your social media campaign, you will first need to look at what is working and what is not. Use metrics such as measurements for engagement, reach, and conversions, amongst others, to guide your strategy.

Example: HubSpot uses data to continue refining its use of social media. They analyze engagement metrics and customer feedback to optimize their content and posting schedules for maximum impact.

Content Calendar

Planning and scheduling your posts in advance ensures a consistent and well-balanced content flow. A content calendar not only helps with planning but also ensures timely and relevant posts.

Example: The New York Times seems to have a well-organized content calendar, updating very regularly across platforms with timely news and engaging articles—including multimedia content—to keep their target audience informed and entertained.

Here are the strategies that would assist businesses in bettering their social media presence to meet their goals. Real-life business scenarios of companies like Netflix, Coca-Cola, GoPro, and Starbucks testify to the fact that being in the know about your audience, being on-brand, and having great content are important. Leveraging platform features, engaging in real-time, teaming up with influencers, making data-based decisions, and planning with a content calendar will help businesses formulate a strong and effective social media marketing approach.

Engaging with Your Audience and Building Community

Relating and community building around the brand are important for the long-term view. Businesses that are actively engaging with customers have a guaranteed following. Here are some of the ways to engage with an audience and build a community.

It's a way of sharing interactive content such as polls, quizzes, or live Q&A, which, for example, is how Spotify imbibes into their many social media platforms to connect with users. Many times during the week, they make polls or even quizzes about people's music preferences, which engage and motivate their followers. This is not only engaging the audience but also providing some insights into their preferences.

Another way is to encourage user-generated content (UGC). Get customers to share their experiences with your product or service on social media. A good example is Lululemon. This athleisure company encourages clients to post pictures of themselves donning Lululemon wear using the hashtag #thesweatlife. This way, there is an increased sense of community among the brand customers and, at the time, authentic marketing content for the brand.

Responsiveness to comments and messages. Quick answers indicate that you find the words your customer has to say valuable and are concerned about their needs. Excellent customer service for an airline like JetBlue Airways would be providing real-time support for their customers on Twitter. For example, they manage their account and respond to incoming customer questions and messages quickly and adequately resolve the subject of the issue in just a few minutes. Such an active approach has served to win the hearts of JetBlue's customers.

Create online groups or communities that are exclusive and can help customers share experiences by offering each other support. An excellent example of such a brand is the fitness brand Peloton, with its Facebook groups and app. Users keep posting their workout milestones, supporting and motivating each other, and often, they get into challenges. This community feeling will keep the user engaged, and loyalty will follow.

And finally, boost community building with virtual events: You can directly engage with your audience via webinars, live streaming, and virtual meet-ups. Adobe constantly holds virtual events and webinars to show its products and to provide tutorials. And it's during these events that it can engage the customers.

These are strategies that companies use to make deeper connections with their customers. Therefore, this creates a sense of community and enhances customer loyalty and satisfaction. Through consistent and meaningful engagement, businesses achieve long-term success and sustainable growth, with customers feeling valued and connected by the company.

Measuring and Analyzing Social Media Success

Measure and analyze actions to maximize social media marketing benefits. This allows you to find out what works, what doesn't, and how to improve. Include critical metrics to track performance levels, such as reach, impressions, growth in followers, and conversion rates. Master the analytics tools provided on social media platforms, as they can give you insights into your performance.

As an example, let's have a look at how Nike measures and analyses their social media success. Nike uses a very diversified set of metrics to understand their campaign performances. Metrics include the tracking of engagement rates to see how many people are interested in the content brought forth and what is the general sentiment of the brand in the market. This way, Nike can tune or update content and strategies to better connect with its audience.

Another example is Airbnb. They do so by running performance analysis on their posts and ads down to the core. Through analyzing clicks, likes, shares, and comments, Airbnb can determine the content type to which members respond the most. They also monitor what percentage of content viewers act, such as booking a stay. Such a data-driven approach with data helps Airbnb optimize campaigns and improve ROI.

Social media success is a kind of attribute that even a leading name in the inbound marketing field like HubSpot practices. They have comprehensive analytics software to keep track of their social channels. Through this, they generally take measures like lead generation or customer acquisition into account so that an evaluation of effectiveness regarding their strategies is done on social media. This helps leak resources efficiently and gain better results.

Now, these social media measurements and analyses of success will give entrepreneurs essential insights into their marketing endeavors and, in the process, fine-tune the strategies for the improvement of rates of engagement and growth. The critical point is reviewing and adjusting your approach based on these data to keep it relevant and effective.

But one thing that an entrepreneur has to realize is that where business is concerned, not every strategy taken will work perfectly for the latter. But being adaptable and ready to experiment, you can find the ways that best suit your needs. If a strategy is not working out for you, do not get stuck on it; move on to the subsequent one and work on it until you make it. By following and implementing this knowledge and strategies, you can build a robust and engaged community and drive long-term success for your business.

CHAPTER 13:

Harnessing Artificial Intelligence in Entrepreneurship

Now, as we step into this last chapter of this book, we enter one of the most transformative forces that is going to change entrepreneurship in tectonic ways: the cutting-edge world of Artificial Intelligence. The chapter's objective is to introduce you to the vast potential of AI and how you can harness these technologies to propel your business. You will see how AI technologies can streamline operations, enhance decision-making, and create highly personalized customer experiences that drive engagement and loyalty.

AI is an umbrella of technologies: learning, natural language processing, predictive analytics, automation, and a whole lot more. Knowing how these can be applied in business helps gain tremendous competitive advantage. This chapter takes you through some efficient approaches to implementing AI in your entrepreneurial venture. From leveraging the full potential of marketing strategies to more effective customer service, automating mundane daily tasks, to data mining for deep insights into the business that have been left unexploited.

You will learn, by exploring the capabilities of AI, to identify and implement those AI solutions that align best with your business objectives and navigate the ethical considerations and possible challenges in AI adoption. Now, you can unlock new levels of efficiency and innovation, positioning your business at the forefront of your industry by embracing AI.

As AI will serve as such a catalyst for growth, this chapter will empower you to change business operations and strategy with the power of artificial intelligence to have sustainable success in this ever-changing entrepreneurial playing field. Get your mind ready to delve deep into the fantastic world of AI and just how it can become part of your entrepreneurial toolkit.

The Role of AI in Modern Business

AI has become an integral part of modern business, transforming various industries through the automation of processes, increased productivity, and, most essentially, enabling the possibility of data-driven decision-making. It helps analyze vast volumes of data within a short period and offers businesses insights that used to remain otherwise hidden.

For example, in retail, AI manages inventory and predicts demand. Among other things, Amazon uses AI algorithms to make sense of purchase patterns and to predict inventory needs, holding just enough supply to ensure that products do not overstock or stock out. This level of precision keeps Amazon meeting its reputation for reliability and speed in the delivery of products to customers.

In the health sector, AI is developing the diagnosis and care being given to the patients. For example, IBM's Watson depends on artificial intelligence to help doctors diagnose diseases and determine treatment plans. Through medical records and research documents, along with clinical data, Watson can produce thoughtful conclusions that guide a practitioner in a better diagnosis and determine the best possible way to proceed with treatment.

AI has also brought in transformation in the financial services. Banks and investment firms apply AI in fraud detection by studying patterns of transactions and pointing out anomalies. Legal documents are scanned using AI in the JP Morgan COIN platform to find essential terms, again saving time and cost by eliminating manual work.

Another perfect case in point is that of customer service. Typically, companies use AI chatbots to handle customer inquiries. Such chatbots answer questions, give information, and solve a few common issues at the same time—all the while learning from each interaction so that they can appropriately solve the next. For instance, Sephora uses AI chatbots to offer personalized beauty advice to customers on what they can use based on their needs and preferences.

This is illustrative of what a transformational role AI plays in the current business world: it empowers an entity, through automation of routine processes, deep insights, and enrichment of interactions, to execute and operate efficiently and effectively. With time, as technology progresses by itself, its impact will only increase within a broad diversity of industries, providing more and more opportunities for innovation and the discovery of ways to do things better.

AI Tools and Technologies for Entrepreneurs

Entrepreneurs today are exposed to most of the available AI tools and technologies that make operations, decision-making, and growth much more accessible. Here are some of the best artificial intelligence tools, along with their capabilities and how they can be used in business:

1. **ChatGPT:** OpenAI's ChatGPT is a powerful language model for understanding and generation of people-like text, which can be applied to customer service, content creation, and virtual assistant jobs. Using the website is a way for the entrepreneur to automatically handle customer inquiries, write an interesting blog post, or perform tedious activities to save time and improve efficiency.

2. **Salesforce Einstein:** This is the other artificial intelligence-based CRM offering on its platform. It deals in predictive analytics, natural language, and machine learning in an attempt to offer insight into the behavior and preferences of the customer. An entrepreneur can use Einstein to predict trends in sales and, in real-time, automate the follow-up of customers while personalizing marketing campaigns to increase customer satisfaction and, in turn, more sales.

3. **Tableau:** This is the most powerful and #1 business intelligence tool on the planet, used to assist any organization in making heaps of data helpful information. Analytics work with artificial intelligence and, through the sifting of big datasets, identify patterns, trends, and outliers. For the entrepreneur, it enables the development of real-time interactive dashboards for better

information on key performance indicators and data-driven decisions to optimize operations/strategies.

4. **Hootsuite Insights:** An AI-powered social media monitoring tool, Hootsuite Insights analyzes social media conversations to derive insights into customer sentiment, emerging trends, and brand perception. Entrepreneurs can use Hootsuite Insights to trace their brand presence online, engage their audience better, and adjust their social media strategy based on real-time data.

5. **HubSpot:** It is an inbound marketing and sales platform with integrated artificial intelligence to increase functionality. It applies lead-scoring, email marketing, and customer-segmentation touchpoints from artificial intelligence. The entrepreneur, armed with HubSpot, will be able to use automated marketing tasks, personalize customer interaction, and manage sales pipelines much more effectively.

6. **IBM Watson:** It is a highly versatile AI platform that supports many tools for aspects related to natural language processing, machine learning, and data analysis. Entrepreneurs, therefore, find a way of developing custom AI applications, undertaking the study of unstructured data, and, in the worst case, even creating chatbots. It is customizable to the particular business use at hand so that it provides insight and automates complicated tasks.

7. **Zoho CRM:** This software has AI in the form of an assistant named Zia, which predicts sales, carries out sentiment analysis, and does workflow automation. An entrepreneur using Zoho CRM can streamline the sales process, get insights into the

engagement of customers, and automate routine tasks that will eventually result in productivity and sales performance.

8. **Crimson Hexagon:** A consumer insights platform powered by AI, it analyzes information sources, including social media data and surveys, to extract consumer feedback. Entrepreneurs can utilize Crimson Hexagon to gain insights into the competitive landscape, consumer preferences, and market trends for informed decision-making in business.

These AI tools and technologies offer a wide range of functionalities that help entrepreneurs achieve performance improvements in business operations. The application of the tools allows entrepreneurs to automate various tasks, gain insights into the business, and finally make data-driven decisions with a vision of efficiency and business growth. Embracing AI technology is crucial to remain competitive and foster innovation in an ever-changing and rapidly evolving business context.

Enhancing Decision-Making with AI

Let's cut down to the chase. This is how—using real-life examples—AI is improving decision-making.

AI enables one to make decisions quickly and correctly after analyzing large volumes of data. For instance, in the business finance sector, AI algorithms are used to analyze market trends and set future direction for stock prices. BlackRock—one of the most significant investment management firms in the world—applies AI-driven systems that allow it to scan massive datasets in search of hidden opportunities and risk management. This will, hence, enable BlackRock to make exact and knowledgeable decisions that will improve the investment strategy and gain returns for the clients.

AI helps retail firms overview consumers' behavior and preferences—what they like and don't. This allows them to make informed decisions about their marketing and inventory. For instance, Starbucks uses its AI-powered tool called Deep Brew to predict purchasing patterns based on deep data analytics from customers. This way, it could have well-tailored marketing efforts, efficient inventory management, and even advice on new store locations. With increasing data-driven decision-making, customer satisfaction increases, driving sales for Starbucks.

Another area in which the impact of artificial intelligence on the process of decision-making has been immense is healthcare. Artificial intelligence is used within hospitals and clinics to analyze patient data for betterment in diagnostics and in proposing treatment plans. For example, the Mayo Clinic utilizes artificial intelligence to obtain information from patient records and research data to identify the best treatment protocols. This allows for more precise diagnosis through personalized treatment plans that result in the desired patient outcome and better operation efficiency. This allows for more accurate diagnoses and personalized treatment plans, affecting excellent patient outcomes and operational efficiency.

AI can potentially optimize supply chain management in the logistics industry by predicting demand, managing inventory, and improving delivery routes. For instance, UPS sustains delivery route optimization through AI through its ORION system, which helps its drivers choose the most efficient routes after considering IMS data of traffic patterns, weather conditions, and the most effective times to deliver. Such data-driven or evidence-based decisions increase operational efficiency and customer satisfaction.

AI also features very widely in human resources as it helps companies make better decisions about hiring and managing talent. IBM uses AI to analyze résumés and make predictions on candidate success while diving into any skill gaps within its workforce. This can allow IBM to streamline the recruiting processes, reduce bias, and ensure it gets the best possible talent for its needs.

These examples prove how AI supports decision-making, providing deep insights, predictive outcomes, and process optimization. AI can help a business venture to strategically and knowingly make more informed decisions, hence driving business growth. With AI, the business is better positioned in the competitive marketplace and able to keep pace with change, thus creating an environment more apt for decision-making based on solid data analysis.

AI for Customer Insights and Personalization

Now, let us discuss how AI can become the ultimate solution in customer insight and deliver personalization. This might be because it can consume vast amounts of data relating to customers, including customer browsing behavior, purchase history, and interaction patterns. The information gives insight into what a business's target audience likes, prefers, acts on, and needs. With such insights, businesses could compose their marketing strategies, product recommendations, and customer interactions to be much more relevant and engaging for the customers. Customization at this level reinforces customer satisfaction and keeps the loyalty rate high, thus helping the business to grow.

One of the most striking examples of AI-driven personalization is Netflix. It processes all the data viewers provide regarding their watching habits, preferences, and ratings by applying AI algorithms. All this information is then returned to the viewer in the form of suggested shows and movies, thus keeping them engaged and satisfied. It goes as far as creating customer thumbnails to ensure that they are presented in a way that best suits each user. That not only assures a perfect user experience but, more importantly, boosts viewership and retention rates to a maximum over any other platform.

Moreover, AI at Amazon drips with customer insight and personalization. With an AI-driven recommendation engine, it understands what customers have been browsing and purchasing in the past to recommend things that might interest them. Such personalized recommendations make up a considerable portion of Amazon's sales, thus showing how AI can engage customers and onboard sales effectively. Alexa from Amazon also uses AI to provide personalized shopping assistance and make a customer's experience hassle-free and customized. Besides, Amazon's Alexa uses AI to provide personalized shopping assistance, making the customer experience convenient and tailored.

For instance, Stitch Fix utilizes AI to provide personalized styling services within the fashion industry. The algorithms use customer profile, style preference, and feedback data to recommend clothing items that match individual styles. This makes the customers more comfortable with this approach, which maximizes personalization of the service, hence leading to low rates of returns since they will tend to keep what fits their taste.

Spotify uses AI for personalized playlists. It uses AI to analyze the patterns of genre preferences, time of the day, etc., to build users' playlists, feeding them this analysis in their Discover Weekly and Daily Mixes. And that much personalization grabs the attention and gets the user to discover more music they would want to listen to.

For example, Sephora, a retailer, uses AI to provide its clients with more personalized beauty recommendations. Sephora utilizes AI with its Virtual Artist app to analyze selfies and recommend make-up products that match the user's skin tone and preferences. It also uses AI in offering personalized skin care advice to customers based on their inputs to better the shopping experience.

In this context, AI illustrates how it will change business in terms of understanding and engaging with the customer. AI enables companies to provide tailored, more personalized experiences to enhance customer relationships and ultimately ensure sustainable success.

Ethical Considerations and Challenges of AI

Noticeably, the more AI is currently being integrated into business operations, the more relevant the question becomes of ethical considerations and challenges one has to deal with it applies. Though

AI has many advantages, it also poses several risks that have to be contracted and judicially governed in terms of fairness, privacy, and transparency.

Another major ethical issue is bias within AI algorithms. Given that AI systems undergo training using data, any form of bias in these data is transferred or even amplified, in effect, towards the AI. For instance, Amazon faced an essential problem with its AI recruitment tool: it was biased against women. The system was trained based on resumes received over ten years, reflecting that the tech industry was dominated by males. This meant that the AI leaned toward male candidates. Amazon has axed the tool and is taking a refreshed approach to AI in hiring.

Another critical issue associated with AI systems is privacy. Most AI systems use vast amounts of data, ordinarily personal in nature; therefore, the security and consent from the users are significant concerns. For example, the case of Facebook and Cambridge Analytica shows how user data was misused. A personal data-based consulting firm, Cambridge Analytica, accessed millions of private data from Facebook users without explicit consent for their political ad targeting services. This case raised awareness regarding more strict data privacy regulations and better transparency in data practices.

Another major challenge is the assurance of transparency in AI decision-making. Most AI systems are "black box" systems that arrive at decisions opaquely. Some of the implications of this could be distrust and problems with accountability. For instance, in the financial sector, AI algorithms approve or disapprove loan applications. This may lead to injustice concerning applicants if such decisions are not reasoned out, and it can also dent the relationship of trust between applicants and the concerned financial institution. Efforts are being made to develop explainable AI that provides insights into how decisions are made. Such opaque decision-making processes can lead to unfair treatment of the applicants and lower their degree of trust in the institutions. The research being conducted is on developing explainable AI (XAI) for decision-making that is used to build trust and accountability.

Another debatable issue is the impact AI has on employment. Though adding to efficiency and productivity, AI may displace jobs at the same time. Automation of manufacturing and customer service can lead to massive job loss involving tasks. Companies, among others, like Walmart, are investing in AI and robotic mechanisms to automate the different processes within their structure. Thus, the future of work for most employees can be a concern. Businesses need to consider the social implications that emanate from the diffusion of AI, and retraining and upskilling programs need investment to transition to new roles.

Finally, making sure that artificial intelligence is adequately used and ethically toward decision-making processes is achieved through clear guidelines and frameworks of artificial intelligence use, periodical audits of artificial intelligence systems, and involvement of diverse teams in artificial intelligence development to mitigate bias and ensure fairness. For example, Google has an AI ethics board that oversees its AI projects to ensure they fall within set guidelines.

Practical Advice for Entrepreneurs:

Start Small

o **Identifying Simple Use Cases:** Start by finding specific, manageable areas where AI can add immediate value. For example, it might help to start with the area of automating customer support through chatbots or using essential AI tools for the analysis of customer data.

o **Pilot Projects:** Bring pilot projects to reality for the testing of AI applications. This way, people will understand how AI integrates with existing processes without much risk or investment.

o **Measure Results:** Evaluate the impact of such micro-projects. Measure metrics with the help of which you can easily find effectiveness enhancement, cost reduction, and improvement in customer satisfaction that AI is bringing to the business.

Invest in Training

o **Employee Education:** Conduct training sessions and workshops for your team to improve AI literacy. To do this, you can take advantage of online classes provided by Coursera, Udemy, and edX.

o **Hands-On Experience:** Let the employees work on AI projects—they pick up practical experience. This can be achieved with the help of internal hackathons or AI-related tasks.

o **Stay Updated:** With AI Journals, webinars, and AI conferences, it will be easy to do continuous learning to keep your team updated with the latest advancements and applications of AI.

Leverage Cloud-Based AI

o **Cost-effective Solutions:** Cloud-based Artificial Intelligence, for example, AWS AI, Google Cloud AI, and Microsoft Azure AI, are cost-effective, as they are scalable without the need for huge capital outlay in infrastructure.

o **Ease of Integration:** Cloud-based AI tools can be easily integrated into your existing systems. They offer APIs and SDKs that ease the implementation process.

o **Access to advanced technologies:** These platforms come with machine learning, natural language processing, and computer vision, which allows you to leverage advanced capabilities without an extended amount of development work.

Collaborate with Experts

o **AI Consultants**: Engage AI consultants or firms that deal with AI to help you with the implementation. They can guide you on how to determine the best use cases and the choice of the right tools, avoiding common pitfalls.

o **Partnerships**: Collaborate with tech firms skilled in artificial intelligence, universities, research, or technology companies.

o **Internal Experts**: Where possible, get an expert in AI or a data scientist; this professional would be invaluable in designing and implementing AI strategies that fit your business needs.

Focus on Ethics

o **Ethical Guidelines**: An organization must develop clear ethical guidelines on AI use. This applies to transparency in AI decision-making, maintenance of data privacy, and free biases in AI algorithms.

o **Regular Audits**: Continually carry out the auditing process for your AI systems to ensure their operation is fair and transparent. This helps you identify and thus mitigate any unintended biases or errors.

o **Customer Trust**: Make AI usage transparent to the consumer. Handle their data responsibly with explicit consent to enhance trust and drive loyalty.

Taking small and careful steps, investing in training, purchasing cloud-based solutions, collaborative processes with specialists, and putting ethical considerations right at the very top to develop an entrepreneurial approach to integrate AI into its business activities successfully. This, quite possibly, could be a way to decrease the risks, ensure the responsible use of AI, and maximize the benefits this technology brings to your organization.

Resources for Getting Started

Online Courses

o **Coursera:** They provide many courses in AI and machine learning from the world's foremost universities and companies. Highlights include "Machine Learning" from Stanford, taught by Andrew Ng, and a course entitled "AI for Everyone," which introduces the basics of artificial intelligence and its applications without getting into the nitty-gritty.

o **Udemy:** There are many courses at different levels relating to AI on this platform. Courses like "Deep Learning A-Z™: Hands-On Artificial Neural Networks" go from basic to very advanced levels and have practical exercises that would allow somebody to apply such knowledge.

o **edX:** Courses are hosted by institutes like MIT and Harvard. The professional certificate program, "Artificial Intelligence," by Columbia University, discusses principles and applications of AI along with some hands-on projects and real-world case studies.

AI Tools

I have already explained the AI tools, but now I will directly share the three most popular and best in the market to get you started.

o **ChatGPT:** This is an application developed by OpenAI that comes with a versatile language model, which allows it to be tuned to whichever application, be it customer service or content generation. It can be plugged into other applications to answer messages automatically and generate human-like text.

o **Salesforce Einstein:** This CRM is AI-powered; it brings predictive analytics, natural language processing, and machine learning. With that, it retains predictive customer intelligence, sales performance optimization, marketing campaign automation and personalization.

o **Tableau:** This is the data visualization resource that uses AI to give in-depth findings on business data. It helps entrepreneurs create interactive dashboards, analyze trends, and make data-driven decisions.

Industry Reports

o **Gartner:** Provides deep reports and analytics on AI trends, technologies, and best practices. Its "Hype Cycle for Artificial Intelligence" gives a graphic take on AI maturity and adoption across various industries.

o **McKinsey:** Publishes insightful research on the impact of AI on business. Their "Global AI Survey" is an industry-agnostic survey, in addition to industry-specific reports, providing valuable data and recommendations on how to use AI in businesses.

o **Forrester:** The AI technologies market research and analysis for the business implication, making their reports possible and more accessible for the business to understand the landscape of AI, and through this help make the right decisions about investments in artificial intelligence.

Community Forums

o **Reddit (r/artificial):** A community of passionate AI professionals and researchers who discuss the latest achievements, share their resources and experiences and support each other. It's a great place to ask questions, learn from others, and stay updated on AI developments.

o **LinkedIn Groups:** Join some AI-focused groups. For example, join "Artificial Intelligence & Machine Learning," where professionals often share various articles, insights, and job opportunities. Such discussions can help entrepreneurs network and view AI from different perspectives.

o **AI Alignment Forum:** This is where the technical and philosophical challenges with ensuring artificial intelligence is friendly to humanity are debated. Valid for an entrepreneur interested in the ethical and safety aspects of artificial intelligence related to its development and deployment.

These resources can empower entrepreneurs with knowledge and instruments to apply AI in business practice. Online courses serve as an initial grounding and advanced understanding of the said discipline; AI tools serve as practical applications; industry reports are set to keep the entrepreneur abreast of trends and best practices; and community forums help with networking and unending learning.

CLOSING:

The Exciting Journey to Business Success

In closing remarks, it is recommended that you teach your employees to be independent thinkers. Teaching your workers how to be independent thinkers is crucial for fostering a culture of innovation, creativity, and growth within your organization. When staff members are equipped to think independently and with the right support, they feel much more involved, encouraged, and valued at their jobs. In addition, it liberates time for leaders to concentrate on higher-level jobs, understanding that their staff members can make informed choices.

It is also important to note that the focus within the business sector is shifting towards sustainability. There is a lot being said about the relevance of environmental, social and governance (ESG) factors in making business decisions. This is a key consideration irrespective of the size of structure of your business. In light of this, it is important that entrepreneurs begin to think in this direction.

While this concept may appear far-fetched, especially for people who are just starting out in their entrepreneurial journey or are in their early days, the truth is that businesses that embed ESG in their core values are better positioned to align their businesses with the shifting expectations of stakeholders and the market at large.

When developing products or services, a key consideration should be whether these products or services are eco- friendly or will increase the carbon footprints across the globe. This is a lot more than climate change activism; it is about recognizing that investors are more likely to request an audit of your operations and may only want to invest in products or services that they consider will not cause significant harm to the environment. This will often require that you leverage technologies to optimize your operations.

Further, it is advisable that you ensure participants within your supply chain do not violate any relevant laws or regimes, as this may create a risk for you. For instance, if the supplier of your raw materials uses children to work at the factory, farm, or any other production site, you may be seen as an accomplice. It is, therefore, important that you develop ethical business practices that respect the rights of individuals and contribute to the advancement of society at large. For emphasis, child labor is just one out of many social issues that a company may be found liable for, and while this book is not focused on social issues, it is important to note that in developing an entrepreneurial mindset, business owners must be aware of these issues and how they may impact profits and returns.

When it comes to governance, we have spoken at length about the value of mentors, employees, peers, and stakeholders. The goal has been to emphasize the need for people. Yet, you must be willing and able to set clear governance structures in place. This will involve developing policies and putting them out there for stakeholders and employees to understand what is required of them as participants within your ecosystem. It will also involve filing relevant reports with the regulatory authorities, among others. You should not start a business with the aim of avoiding taxes or other regulatory obligations because that will work to your disadvantage in the long run.

Indeed, there are a lot of challenges, regulatory complexities, and resource constraints within the business sector. This you will encounter when implementing the strategies and principles in this book. However, your ability to overcome these challenges is crucial to building a sustainable and successful business.

About the Author

Meet Lena Voss, a successful businesswoman, talented writer, and academic researcher who lends a career with a total of experience and insights into how to be successful in the world of business. Having had the chance to work in various industries and numerous companies across the globe enabled this very author to develop a sense and feel for what allows some organizations to be successful in the modern competitive markets.

Lena is a treasure trove of experiences, with valuable lessons learned and practical advice gained from many years. Starting right from how to encourage independent thinking in your subordinates to embracing ESG principles, Lena guides readers on developing a sustainable business that thrives on innovation.

With a passion for empowering entrepreneurs and business leaders, Lena explores key strategies for overcoming challenges, navigating regulatory complexities, and leveraging technology to optimize operations. Through engaging storytelling and actionable insights, this book offers a roadmap to achieving long-term success while making a positive impact on society.

Join Lena Voss on this exciting journey to business success and learn how to make a thriving enterprise attuned to the changing stakes of the stakeholders and the market in general.

Acknowledgments

It has been a fantastic journey to write this book, and I want to thank everyone who helped me on my way. First and foremost, I would like to thank my family. Your relentless encouragement and love kept me going. Your patience and understanding in the forever-long and countless hours that I put into writing this book truly made it possible for me to do so.

Special thanks also go to my colleagues and mentors in the business world: your many insights, advice, and sharing of experiences shaped my understanding of how to succeed. Most importantly, I would like to acknowledge those who took the time to review drafts and give me valuable feedback.

I would like to acknowledge the great team at my publishing house. Your experience, creativity, and dedication are all those things that have worked tirelessly to bring this book to life. Thank you for believing in my vision and helping put a refined touch to it.

My friends and peers, thanks for the continuous support and enthusiasm. Knowing that you all had belief in me kept me going through the ups and downs during my writing process.

Last but not least, I would genuinely like to express my heartfelt gratitude to the readers. Your interest and passion for the new business model for sustainability are precisely what brought this book into existence. May the ideas presented within empower you with a zeal that fuels success. Thank you all for joining me on this exciting journey.

Bibliography

Acton, C. (2022). Are you aware of your biases? Harvard Business Review. https://hbr.org/2022/02/are-you-aware-of-your-biases

Ajzen, I. (1991). The theory of planned behavior. Organizational Behavior and Human Decision Processes, 50(2), 179-211. https://doi.org/10.1016/0749-5978(91)90020-T

Akbar, K., & Ayandibu, A. (2022). Creativity and innovation: The need for cognitive skills and abilities in developing entrepreneurs of the future. In Achieving Sustainability Using Creativity, Innovation, and Education: A Multidisciplinary Approach (pp. 18). IGI Global. https://doi.org/10.4018/978-1-7998-7963-3.ch003

Akehurst, G., Comeche, J. M., & Galindo, M.-A. (2009). Job satisfaction and commitment in the entrepreneurial SME. Small Business Economics, 32(3), 277-289. https://doi.org/10.1007/s11187-008-9116-z

American Psychological Association. (n.d.). Stress effects on the body. APA Topics. Retrieved August 27, 2023, from https://www.apa.org/topics/stress/body

Anderson, N., Potočnik, K., & Zhou, J. (2014). Innovation and creativity in organizations: A state-of-the-science review, prospective commentary, and guiding framework. Journal of Management, 40(5), 1297-1333. https://doi.org/10.1177/0149206314527128

Bailey, R. R. (2019). Goal setting and action planning for health behavior change. American Journal of Lifestyle Medicine, 13(6), 615-618. https://doi.org/10.1177/1559827617729634

Baumeister, R. F., & Tierney, J. (2011). Willpower: Rediscovering the greatest human strength. Penguin.

Belyh, A. (2022). Meet the top 12 most innovative entrepreneurs of 2023. FounderJar. https://www.founderjar.com/most-innovative-entrepreneurs/

Bravata, D. M., Watts, S. A., Keefer, A. L., Madhusudhan, D. K., Taylor, K. T., Clark, D. M., Nelson, R. S., Cokley, K. O., & Hagg, H. K. (2019). Prevalence, predictors, and treatment of impostor syndrome: A systematic review. Journal of General Internal Medicine, 34(9), 2000-2007. https://doi.org/10.1007/s11606-019-05364-1

Brehm, J. (1966). A theory of psychological reactance. Academic Press.

Carver, C. S., Scheier, M. F., & Weintraub, J. K. (1989). Assessing coping strategies: A theoretically based approach. Journal of Personality and Social Psychology, 56(2), 267-283.

Cater, J. J., III, Young, M., & Hua, L. (2023). Examining the entrepreneurial mindset and entrepreneurial intentions. The Journal of Applied Business and Economics. https://doi.org/10.33423/jabe.v25i4.6339

Chen, H., Pang, L., Liu, F., Fang, T., & Wen, Y. (2022). "Be perfect in every respect": The mediating role of career adaptability in the relationship between perfectionism and career decision-making difficulties of college students. BMC Psychology, 10(1), 137. https://doi.org/10.1186/s40359-022-00845-1

Chen, Y. (2012). Research on the evolution of enterprise routines: Motives, paths and model construction. Journal of Business Economics.

Cherry, K. (2023). What is the fear of success? VeryWell Mind. https://www.verywellmind.com/what-is-the-fear-of-success-5179184

Čigarská, B. N., & Birknerová, Z. (2021). Assessment of selected determinants of burnout syndrome and coping strategies in terms of gender in entrepreneurs. Psychology and Education Bulletin, 2(1), 24-31. https://doi.org/10.12955/PEB.V2.251

Covey, S. R. (1989). The 7 habits of highly effective people: Restoring the character ethic. Free Press.

Csíkszentmihályi, M. (1975). Beyond boredom and anxiety: The experience of play in work and games. Jossey-Bass.

Clance, P. R., & Imes, S. A. (1978). The impostor phenomenon in high achieving women: Dynamics and therapeutic intervention. Psychotherapy: Theory, Research & Practice, 15(3), 241-247.

Clance, P. R. (1985). The impostor phenomenon: Overcoming the fear that haunts your success. Peachtree Publishers.

Day, T., & Tosey, P. (2011). Beyond SMART? A new framework for goal setting. Curriculum Journal, 22(4), 515-534. https://doi.org/10.1080/09585176.2011.627213

Diener, C. I., & Dweck, C. S. (1978). An analysis of learned helplessness: Continuous changes in performance, strategy, and achievement cognitions following failure. Journal of Personality and Social Psychology, 36(5), 451-462.

Doran, G. T. (1981). There's a S.M.A.R.T. way to write management's goals and objectives. Management Review, 70(11), 35-36.

Dweck, C. S. (2006). Mindset: The new psychology of success. Random House.

Eccles, J. S., & Wigfield, A. (2002). Motivational beliefs, values, and goals. Annual Review of Psychology, 53(1), 109-132.

Eddleston, K., Ladge, J., & Sugiyama, K. (2020). 'Imposter syndrome' holds back entrepreneurial women. Entrepreneur and Innovation Exchange. https://doi.org/10.32617/438-5e4bda061a20d

Editorial Team BetterHelp. (2024). What Are Dopamine Pathways And How Do They Work?. BetterHelp.

https://www.betterhelp.com/advice/medication/what-are-dopamine-pathways-and-how-do-they-work/

Eysenck, M. W., & Calvo, M. G. (1992). Anxiety and performance: The processing efficiency theory. Cognition & Emotion, 6(6), 409-434.

Faure, A., Reynolds, S. M., Richard, J. M., & Berridge, K. C. (2008). Mesolimbic dopamine in desire and dread: Enabling motivation to be generated by localized glutamate disruptions in nucleus accumbens. Journal of Neuroscience, 28(28), 7184-7192. https://doi.org/10.1523/JNEUROSCI.4961-07.2008

Fotios, V., Mitsakis. (2020). Human resource development (HRD) resilience: a new 'success element' of organizational resilience? Human Resource Development International, 23(3), 321-328. https://doi.org/10.1080/13678868.2019.1669385

Friedman, D., Pommerenke, K., Lukose, R., Milam, G., & Huberman, B. A. (2007). Searching for the sunk cost fallacy. Experimental Economics, 10, 79-104. https://doi.org/10.1007/s10683-006-9134-0

Gadd, K. W. (1995). Business self-assessment. Business Process Management Journal, 1(3), 66-85. https://doi.org/10.1108/EUM0000000003894

Garn, R. (2023). How to leverage AI to supercharge your business. Entrepreneur. https://www.entrepreneur.com/science-technology/how-to-leverage-ai-to-supercharge-your-business/466194

GEM. (2024). Global press release. GEM Global Entrepreneurship Monitor. https://www.gemconsortium.org/reports/latest-global-report

Gibson, J. (2019). Mindfulness, interoception, and the body: A contemporary perspective. Frontiers in Psychology, 10, 2012. https://doi.org/10.3389/fpsyg.2019.02012

Gollwitzer, P. M. (1999). Implementation intentions: Strong effects of simple plans. American Psychologist, 54(7), 493-503.

Gonzales, A. M., Lin, J.-H., & Cha, J. S. (2022). Promoting healthier office environments: Evaluation of mindfulness and gym interventions. Proceedings of the Human Factors and Ergonomics Society Annual Meeting, 66(1), 497-497. https://doi.org/10.1177/1071181322661230

Gordon, R. M. (1987). The structure of emotions. Cambridge University Press.

Helms, M. M., & Nixon, J. (2010). Exploring SWOT analysis – where are we now? A review of academic research from the last decade. Journal of Strategy and Management, 3(3), 215-251. https://doi.org/10.1108/17554251011064837

Horner, M. S. (1968). Success and women. Doctoral dissertation, University of Michigan.

Hu, B., Zheng, Q., Wu, J., Tang, Z., Zhu, J., Wu, S., & Ling, Y. (2021). Role of education and mentorship in entrepreneurial behavior: Mediating role of self-efficacy. Frontiers in Psychology, 12. https://doi.org/10.3389/fpsyg.2021.775227

Humphrey, A. (2005). SWOT analysis for management consulting. SRI Alumni Association Newsletter, SRI International.

Hunt, J. (2020). Unlocking Your Authentic Self: Overcoming Imposter Syndrome, Enhancing Self-Confidence, and Banishing Self-Doubt. John Hunt Publishing.

Hwang, K., & Choi, J. (2021). How do failed entrepreneurs cope with their prior failure when they seek subsequent re-entry into serial entrepreneurship? Failed entrepreneurs' optimism and defensive pessimism and coping humor as a moderator. International Journal of Environmental Research and Public Health, 18(13), 7021. https://doi.org/10.3390/IJERPH18137021

Janis, I. L. (1972). Victims of Groupthink: A Psychological Study of Foreign-Policy Decisions and Fiascoes. Houghton Mifflin.

Joel, M., & Shulman, J. (2019). Entrepreneurs breed ESG-rich companies: Reap exceptional returns as harvest byproduct. The Journal of Index Investing, 9(4), 18-45. https://doi.org/10.3905/JII.2019.1.065

Johnson, D. D. P., & Fowler, J. H. (2011). The evolution of overconfidence. Nature, 477(7364), 317-320. https://doi.org/10.1038/nature10384

Karabenick, S. A. (2023). On the rewards of being open to opportunities and their challenges. In T. Urdan & E. N. Gonida (Eds.), Remembering the Life, Work, and Influence of Stuart A. Karabenick (Advances in Motivation and Achievement, Vol. 22) (pp. 7-24). Emerald Publishing Limited. https://doi.org/10.1108/S0749-742320230000022002

Klein, H. J., Wesson, M. J., Hollenbeck, J. R., & Alge, B. J. (1999). Goal commitment and the goal-setting process: Conceptual clarification and empirical synthesis. Journal of Applied Psychology, 84(6), 885-896. https://doi.org/10.1037/0021-9010.84.6.885

Korte, R., Smith, K. A., & Li, C. Q. (2018). The role of empathy in entrepreneurship: A core competency of the entrepreneurial mindset. Advances in Engineering Education, 7(1).

Larsen, I., & Blenker, P. (2023). The entrepreneurial mindset in entrepreneurship education: What can we learn from S-O-R models? Journal of Education and Training. https://doi.org/10.1108/ET-09-2022-0364

Leadem, R. (2017). 12 leaders, entrepreneurs, and celebrities who have struggled with imposter syndrome. Entrepreneur. https://www.entrepreneur.com/leadership/12-leaders-entrepreneurs-and-celebrities-who-have/304273

Li, Y., Cao, K., & Jenatabadi, H. S. (2023). Effect of entrepreneurial education and creativity on entrepreneurial intention in college students: Mediating entrepreneurial inspiration, mindset, and self-efficiency. Frontiers in Psychology. https://doi.org/10.3389/fpsyg.2023.1240910

Locke, E. A., & Latham, G. P. (1990). A theory of goal setting & task performance. Prentice-Hall.

Locke, E. A., & Latham, G. P. (2002). Building a practically useful theory of goal setting and task motivation: A 35-year odyssey. American Psychologist, 57(9), 705-717.

Manoharan, C., Arivazhagan, D., Divyaranjani, R., & Vetri, S. R. (2020). Cognition and emotions during the teaching-learning process. International Journal of Scientific & Technology Research, 9(2), 267-269.

Marmenout, K. (2010). Coaching for work-life balance. In J. Stredwick & S. K. Wise (Eds.), The handbook of human resource management (pp. 217-227). Palgrave Macmillan. https://doi.org/10.1057/9780230281790_14

Marshall, A. (1890). Principles of Economics. Macmillan.

Mather, M., & Sutherland, M. R. (2011). Arousal-biased competition in perception and memory. Perspectives on Psychological Science, 6(2), 114-133.

Mesri, W., Manafe, N., Ohara, R., Gadzali, S. S., Harahap, M. A. K., & Almaududi, A. M. (2023). Exploring the relationship between entrepreneurial mindsets and business success: Implications for entrepreneurship education. Journal on Education, 5(4), 12540-12547. https://doi.org/10.31004/joe.v5i4.2238

Metcalfe, J., & Jacobs, W. J. (1998). Emotional memory: The effects of stress on "cool" and "hot" memory systems. In D. L. Medin (Ed.), The psychology of learning and motivation: Advances in research and theory (Vol. 38, pp. 187-222). Academic Press.

Mishan, E. J., & Quah, E. (2020). Cost-Benefit Analysis (6th ed.). Routledge.

Monica, C. (2022). How resilience influences the organisational success. Theoretical Perspectives on Employee and Managerial Resilience. Revista Romaneasca pentru Educatie Multidimensionala, 14(4 Sup.1), 201-216. https://doi.org/10.18662/rrem/14.4sup1/667

Nate, S., Grecu, V., Stavytskyy, A., & Kharlamova, G. (2022). Fostering entrepreneurial ecosystems through the stimulation and mentorship of new entrepreneurs. Sustainability, 14(13), 7985. https://doi.org/10.3390/su14137985

Nebhwani, M., Marri, H. B., Sohag, R. A., & Ahmed, S. (2011). An assessment of entrepreneurs' business strategies towards SME success. Mehran University Research Journal of Engineering and Technology, 30(3), 469-476.

O'Brien, K., & Cooper, C. (2022). Elgar introduction to organizational stress theories. Edward Elgar Publishing. https://doi.org/10.4337/9781789909838

Orlov, S., & Lugovoy, I. N. (2022). Entrepreneurship's adaptation to the national ESG agenda. Vestnik Tomskogo Gosudarstvennogo Universiteta. Èkonomika, 58, 208-223. https://doi.org/10.17223/19988648/58/13

Panigrahi, A. K. (2021). Managing stress at the workplace. Journal of Management and Research, 3(4), 154-160.

Park, W.-W. (2000). A comprehensive empirical investigation of the relationships among variables of the groupthink model. Journal of Organizational Behavior, 21(8), 873-887. https://doi.org/10.1002/1099-1379(200012)21:8<873::AID-JOB56>3.0.CO;2-8

Pignatiello, G. A., Martin, R. J., & Hickman, R. L. Jr. (2020). Decision fatigue: A conceptual analysis. Journal of Health Psychology, 25(1), 123-135. https://doi.org/10.1177/1359105318763510'

Quinlan, J. R. (1986). Induction of decision trees. Machine Learning, 1(1), 81-106. https://doi.org/10.1007/BF00116251

Reeve, J. (2014). Understanding motivation and emotion (6th ed.). Wiley.

Richardson, J. C., & Chew-Graham, C. A. (2016). Resilience and well-being. In C. Chew-Graham & M. Ray (Eds.), Mental Health and Older People (pp. 21-34). Springer, Cham. https://doi.org/10.1007/978-3-319-29492-6_2

Robbins, S. P., & Judge, T. A. (2013). Organizational Behavior (15th ed.). Prentice Hall.

Robinson, D. A., VanderPal, G., & Hoang, D. N. (2017). Entrepreneurs' leadership experiences with specific regard to mentorship. Journal of Leadership, Accountability, and Ethics, 14(3), 91-100.

Ryan, R. M., & Deci, E. L. (2000). Self-determination theory and the facilitation of intrinsic motivation, social development, and well-being. American Psychologist, 55(1), 68-78.

Saggar, M., Quintin, E.-M., Bott, N., Kienitz, E., Chien, Y.-H., Hong, D., Liu, N., Royalty, A., Hawthorne, G., & Reiss, A. (2016). Changes in brain activation associated with spontaneous improvisation and figural creativity after design-thinking-based training: A longitudinal fMRI study. Cerebral Cortex, 27(4), bhw171. https://doi.org/10.1093/cercor/bhw171

Sattizahn, J. R., Moser, J. S., & Beilock, S. L. (2016). A closer look at who "chokes under pressure". Journal of Applied Research in Memory and Cognition, 5(4), 470-477. https://doi.org/10.1016/j.jarmac.2016.11.004

Schwartz, B. (2004). The Paradox of Choice: Why More Is Less. Harper Perennial.

Schwarz, N., & Vaughn, L. A. (2002). The availability heuristic revisited: Ease of recall and content of recall as distinct sources of information. In T. Gilovich, D. Griffin, & D. Kahneman (Eds.), Heuristics and biases: The psychology of intuitive judgment (pp. 103-119). Cambridge University Press.

Shah, P., & Oppenheimer, D. M. (2008). Heuristics made easy: An effort-reduction framework. Psychological Bulletin, 134(2), 207-222. https://doi.org/10.1037/0033-2909.134.2.207

Shah-Zhou, H., & Bojica, A. M. (2017). The role of emotional intelligence in entrepreneurs' perceptions of success: An exploratory study. Entrepreneurship Research Journal, 15(3), 341-360.

Sheldon, K. M., & Elliot, A. J. (1999). Goal striving, need satisfaction, and longitudinal well-being: The self-concordance model. Journal of Personality and Social Psychology, 76(3), 482-497.

Shi, B., & Wang, T. (2021). Analysis of entrepreneurial motivation on entrepreneurial psychology in the context of transition economy. Frontiers in Psychology. https://doi.org/10.3389/fpsyg.2021.680296

Smith, J., & Doe, A. (2019). The definition of entrepreneurship: Is it less complex than we think? International Journal of Entrepreneurial Behavior & Research, 25(6), 1280-1297. https://doi.org/10.1108/IJEBR-11-2019-0634

Stanislavsky, O. O., Vlasenko, T., Kozak, K., & Demchenko, O. (2023). The development of emotional intelligence as a factor in the success of entrepreneurial activity. Innovation and Sustainability Series, 1, 99-105. https://doi.org/10.31649/ins.2023.1.99.105

St-Jean, E., & Tremblay, M. (2023). Turbulence and adaptations to the coronavirus crisis: Resources, coping, and effects on stress and wellbeing of entrepreneurs. International Entrepreneurship and Management Journal, 1-23. https://doi.org/10.1007/s11365-023-00851-8

Sundari, Johansen, & Hurwitt. (2023). Redefining entrepreneurship: The incorporation of CSR and positive corporate image as business strategies in green entrepreneurialism. In M. B. I. N. Faizal, L.

Sundari, & S. Johansen (Eds.), Environmental footprints and eco-design of products and processes (pp. 147-161). Springer. https://doi.org/10.1007/978-981-19-8895-0_6

Thaler, R. (1980). Toward a positive theory of consumer choice. Journal of Economic Behavior & Organization, 1(1), 39-60.

Tulshyan, R., & Burey, J.-A. (2021, July 14). End imposter syndrome in your workplace. Harvard Business Review. https://hbr.org/2021/07/end-imposter-syndrome-in-your-workplace

Tversky, A., & Kahneman, D. (1973). Availability: A heuristic for judging frequency and probability. Cognitive Psychology, 5(2), 207-232.

Tversky, A., & Kahneman, D. (1974). Judgment under uncertainty: Heuristics and biases. Science, 185(4157), 1124-1131.

U.S. Bureau of Labor Statistics. (n.d.). Blsgov. https://www.bls.gov/bdm/us_age_naics_00_table5.txt

Uğur, G. (2014). The investigation of the resilience and wellness of university students according to some variables. Education Sciences, 9(1), 19-35.

United Nations. (n.d.). Take action for the sustainable development goals. Sustainable Development Goals. https://www.un.org/sustainabledevelopment/sustainable-development-goals/

University of Minnesota Libraries. (2017). 11.2 Understanding decision making. Libraries. https://open.lib.umn.edu/organizationalbehavior/chapter/11-2-understanding-decision-making/

van Berkel, J., Proper, K. I., Boot, C. R. L., Bongers, P. M., & van der Beek, A. J. (2011). Mindful "Vitality in Practice": An intervention to improve the work engagement and energy balance among workers; the development and design of the randomized

controlled trial. BMC Public Health, 11(1), 736.
https://doi.org/10.1186/1471-2458-11-736

Vroom, V. H. (1964). Work and motivation. Wiley.

Wang, A. R., Groome, A., Taniguchi, L., Eshel, N., & Bentzley, B.
S. (2020). The role of dopamine in reward-related behavior: Shining
new light on an old debate. Journal of Neurophysiology, 124(2),
309-311. https://doi.org/10.1152/jn.00323.2020

Warrell, D. M. (2015). Sunk-cost bias: Is it time to call it quits?
Forbes.
https://www.forbes.com/sites/margiewarrell/2015/09/14/sunk-cost-
bias-is-it-time-to-move-on/?sh=30c2ebd53cff

Wason, P. C. (1960). On the failure to eliminate hypotheses in a
conceptual task. Quarterly Journal of Experimental Psychology,
12(3), 129-140.

Wilkinson, A., & Kupers, R. (2013). The Essence of Scenarios:
Learning from the Shell Experience. Amsterdam University Press.

Wilson, S. B., & Dobson, M. S. (2008). Goal Setting: How to Create
an Action Plan and Achieve Your Goals (2nd ed.).

www.ingramcontent.com/pod-product-compliance
Lightning Source LLC
Chambersburg PA
CBHW042124190326
41521CB00017B/2598